ÉDITION FRANÇAISE
ENGLISH
FOR EVERYONE

EXERCICES
NIVEAU 1 DÉBUTANT

T0322234

AUDIO GRATUIT
Site Internet et appli
www.dkefe.com

L'auteur

Thomas Booth a enseigné l'anglais en Pologne et en Russie pendant 10 ans. Il réside désormais en Angleterre, où il travaille en tant qu'éditeur et auteur de matériel d'apprentissage de l'anglais (manuels d'apprentissage et de vocabulaire).

Les consultants pédagogiques

Tim Bowen a enseigné l'anglais et formé des enseignants dans plus de trente pays. Il est le coauteur d'ouvrages sur l'enseignement de la prononciation et sur la méthodologie de l'enseignement des langues, et est l'auteur de nombreux ouvrages pour les enseignants d'anglais. Il travaille actuellement comme auteur indépendant de matériels pédagogique, éditeur et traducteur. Il est membre du Chartered Institute of Linguists.

Kate O'Donovan, irlandaise, est titulaire d'un PDGE, et d'une licence d'histoire et d'anglais. Elle a travaillé en Suisse, à Oman et au Bahreïn. Depuis 2014 à Paris, elle enseigne l'anglais au British Council où elle est aussi coordinatrice.

La consultante linguistique

Susan Barduhn est professeur d'anglais et formatrice expérimentée d'enseignants. Elle a, en tant qu'auteur, contribué à de nombreuses publications. Elle donne non seulement des cours d'anglais dans le monde entier, mais est également présidente de l'Association internationale des professeurs d'anglais langue étrangère et conseillère auprès du Conseil britannique et du département d'État américain. Elle est actuellement professeur à la School for International Training dans le Vermont, aux États-Unis.

ÉDITION FRANÇAISE
ENGLISH
FOR EVERYONE

EXERCICES
NIVEAU 1 DÉBUTANT

Aa

Assistants d'édition Jessica Cawthra, Sarah Edwards
Illustrateurs Edwood Burn, Denise Joos,
Michael Parkin, Jemma Westing
Producteur audio Liz Hammond
Rédacteur en chef Daniel Mills
Éditeur artistique en chef Anna Hall
Gestionnaire de projet Christine Stroyan
Concepteur couverture Natalie Godwin
Éditeur couverture Claire Gell
Responsable conception couverture Sophia MTT
Production, préproduction Luca Frassinetti
Production Mary Slater
Éditeur Andrew Macintyre
Directeur artistique Karen Self
Directeur de publication Jonathan Metcalf

DK Inde
Concepteur couverture Surabhi Wadhwa
Éditeur couvertures en chef Saloni Singh
Concepteur PAO en chef Harish Aggarwal

Publié en Grande-Bretagne en 2016
par Dorling Kindersley Limited
DK, One Embassy Gardens,
8 Viaduct Gardens, London, SW11 7BW

Le représentant autorisé dans l'EEE est
Dorling Kindersley Verlag GmbH. Arnulfstra. 124,
80636 Munich, Allemagne

Titre original : *English For Everyone. Practice Book.*
Level 1. Beginner

Copyright © 2016 Dorling Kindersley Limited
Une société faisant partie du groupe Penguin Random House

Pour la version française :
© 2017 Dorling Kindersley Limited

Adaptation et réalisation : Édiclic
Révision pédagogique : Kate O'Donovan
Traduction : Estelle Demontrond-Box pour Édiclic
Lecture-correction : Paul Cléonie

ISBN : 978-0-2413-0244-6
Imprimé et relié en Slovaquie

Pour les esprits curieux
www.dk.com

Sommaire

Fonctionnement du cours

English for everyone est un ouvrage conçu pour toutes les personnes désireuses d'apprendre l'anglais par elles-mêmes. Comme tout cours de langue, il porte sur les compétences de base : grammaire, vocabulaire, prononciation, compréhension orale, expression orale, compréhension écrite et expression écrite. Ici, les compétences sont enseignées de façon visuelle, à l'aide d'images et de schémas pour vous aider à comprendre et à bien mémoriser. Ce livre d'exercices comprend de nombreux exercices conçus pour renforcer les leçons apprises dans le manuel d'apprentissage. Suivez la progression des chapitres en veillant à utiliser les enregistrements à votre disposition sur le site Internet et l'application.

MANUEL D'APPRENTISSAGE

LIVRE D'EXERCICES

Numéro de chapitre Ce livre d'exercices est divisé en chapitres. Chacun d'eux revient sur les points linguistiques abordés dans le chapitre du manuel d'apprentissage correspondant.

Les points d'apprentissage
Chaque chapitre débute par un résumé des points de pratique clés.

Modules Chaque chapitre est divisé en modules, qui doivent être réalisés dans l'ordre. Vous pouvez faire une pause à la fin de chaque module.

Vocabulaire Tout au long du livre, des pages de vocabulaire évaluent vos connaissances des expressions et mots anglais clés enseignés dans le manuel d'apprentissage.

Pratique visuelle Des images et graphiques vous donnent des indices visuels pour vous aider à mémoriser les mots anglais les plus utiles et les plus importants.

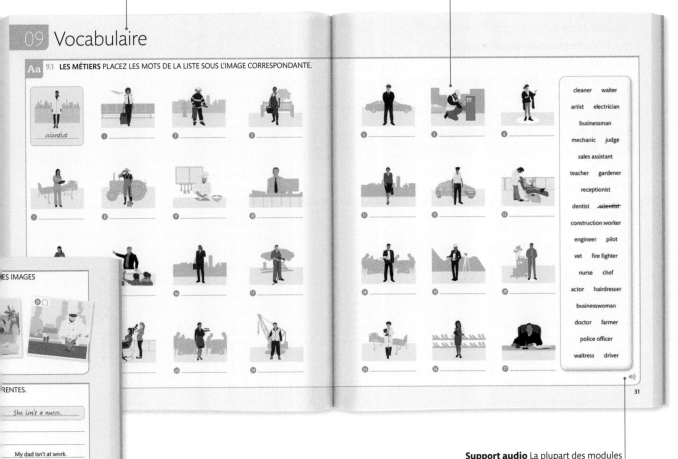

Support audio La plupart des modules sont accompagnés d'enregistrements sonores de locuteurs anglophones pour vous aider à améliorer vos compétences de compréhension et d'expression orales.

AUDIO GRATUIT
Site Internet et appli
www.dkefe.com

Modules d'exercices

Chaque exercice est soigneusement conçu pour mettre en pratique et tester les nouveaux points linguistiques enseignés dans les chapitres correspondants du manuel d'apprentissage. Les exercices accompagnant le manuel vous aideront à mieux mémoriser ce que vous avez appris et donc à mieux maîtriser la langue anglaise. Chaque exercice est introduit par un symbole indiquant la compétence étudiée.

 GRAMMAIRE
Appliquez les règles grammaticales dans des contextes différents.

COMPRÉHENSION ÉCRITE
Étudiez la langue dans des contextes anglophones authentiques.

COMPRÉHENSION ORALE
Évaluez votre niveau de compréhension de l'anglais oral.

 VOCABULAIRE
Consolidez votre compréhension du vocabulaire clé.

EXPRESSION ORALE
Comparez votre anglais oral aux enregistrements audio types.

Numéro de module Chaque module est identifié par un numéro unique qui vous permet de trouver facilement les réponses et les enregistrements associés.

Consignes des exercices
Chaque exercice est introduit par une consigne courte qui vous explique ce que vous devez faire.

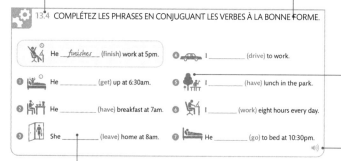

Supports graphiques
Des images ou pictogrammes sont fournis pour vous aider à comprendre les exercices.

Supports audio Ce symbole indique que les réponses de l'exercice sont disponibles sous forme d'enregistrements audio. Écoutez-les une fois l'exercice terminé.

Espace pour écrire
Il est recommandé que vous écriviez vos réponses dans le livre d'exercices pour conserver une trace et évaluer vos résultats.

Exercice de compréhension orale
Ce symbole indique que vous devez écouter un enregistrement audio afin de répondre aux questions de l'exercice.

Exemple de réponse
La réponse des premières questions de chaque exercice vous est donnée pour vous aider à mieux comprendre la consigne.

Exercice d'expression orale Ce symbole indique que vous devez donner les réponses à voix haute, puis que vous devez les comparer aux enregistrements types compris dans les fichiers audio.

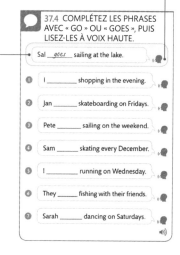

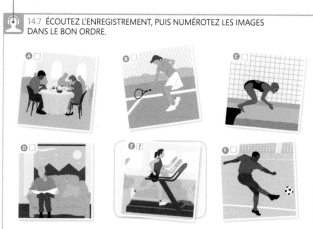

Audio

English for everyone contient de nombreux documents audio. Il vous est recommandé de les utiliser autant que possible, afin d'améliorer votre compréhension de l'anglais parlé et d'avoir un accent et une prononciation plus naturels. Chaque dossier peut être lu, mis en pause ou répété aussi souvent que vous le désirez, jusqu'à ce que vous soyez sûr d'avoir parfaitement compris ce qui a été dit.

EXERCICES DE COMPRÉHENSION ORALE

Ce symbole indique que vous devez écouter un enregistrement afin de pouvoir répondre aux questions d'un exercice.

AUDIO ASSOCIÉ

Ce symbole indique qu'un enregistrement supplémentaire est à votre disposition une fois le module terminé.

AUDIO GRATUIT
Site Internet et appli
www.dkefe.com

Réponses

À la fin du livre d'exercices, une section répertorie toutes les réponses de chaque exercice. Référez-vous à ces pages lorsque vous avez terminé un module, et comparez vos réponses avec celles proposées. Vous pourrez ainsi évaluer si vous avez bien compris chaque point d'apprentissage.

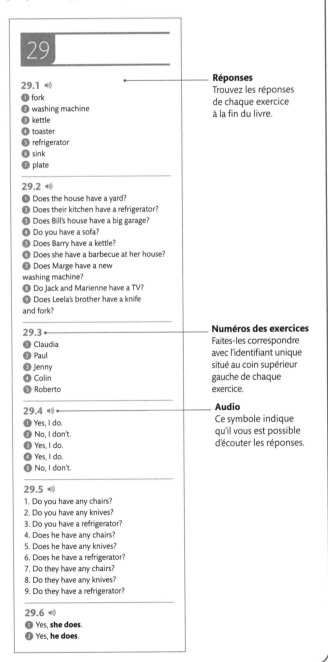

Réponses
Trouvez les réponses de chaque exercice à la fin du livre.

Numéros des exercices
Faites-les correspondre avec l'identifiant unique situé au coin supérieur gauche de chaque exercice.

Audio
Ce symbole indique qu'il vous est possible d'écouter les réponses.

01 Vous présenter

Vous pouvez saluer d'autres personnes en disant « Hello! » ou « Hi! ». Pour vous présenter, dites « I am ». Vous aurez peut-être également besoin d'épeler votre nom.

⚙️ **Grammaire** « To be » pour dire son nom

Aa Vocabulaire Dire votre nom et les lettres de l'alphabet

🧩 **Compétence** Dire votre nom

1.1 RÉCRIVEZ LES PHRASES À LA FORME CONTRACTÉE.

My name is Gary
My name's Gary.

① I am Natalie.

_____

② My name is Sue.

_____

③ I am Ryan.

_____

④ My name is Mia.

_____

⑤ My name is Amelia.

_____

🔊

1.2 ÉCOUTEZ L'ENREGISTREMENT, PUIS REMETTEZ LES PERSONNAGES DANS L'ORDRE.

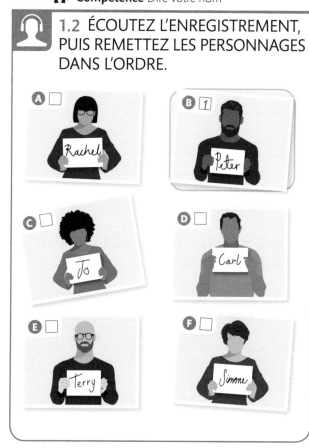

1.3 UTILISEZ LE SCHÉMA POUR CRÉER 12 SALUTATIONS, PUIS LISEZ-LES À VOIX HAUTE.

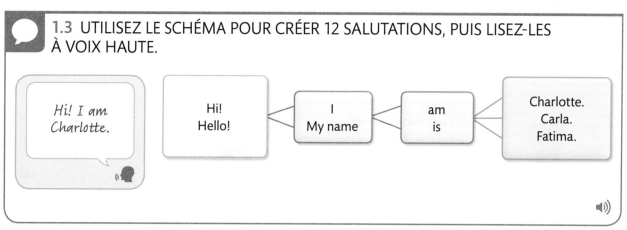

🔊

1.4 ÉCOUTEZ L'ENREGISTREMENT, PUIS ÉCRIVEZ ET ÉPELEZ LES NOMS QUE VOUS ENTENDEZ.

R-A-C-H-E-L   H-A-R-P-E-R

1 _____

2 _____

3 _____

4 _____

5 _____

6 _____

7 _____

8 _____

9 _____

10 _____

11 _____

12 _____

13 _____

14 _____

15 _____

1.5 ÉPELEZ LE NOM DE CHAQUE PERSONNE, PUIS LISEZ LES PHRASES À VOIX HAUTE.

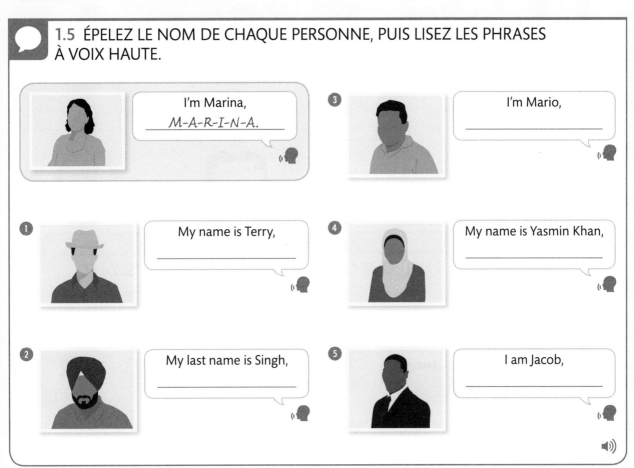

I'm Marina,
M-A-R-I-N-A.

3 I'm Mario,
_____

1 My name is Terry,
_____

4 My name is Yasmin Khan,
_____

2 My last name is Singh,
_____

5 I am Jacob,
_____

Aa **2.1 LES PAYS** ÉCRIVEZ LE NOM DU PAYS CORRESPONDANT À CHAQUE DRAPEAU.

Turkey

1 _____

2 _____

3 _____

4 _____

10 _____

11 _____

12 _____

13 _____

14 _____

20 _____

21 _____

22 _____

23 _____

24 _____

30 _____

31 _____

32 _____

33 _____

34 _____

5 _____

6 _____

7 _____

8 _____

9 _____

15 _____

16 _____

17 _____

18 _____

19 _____

25 _____

26 _____

27 _____

28 _____

29 _____

Republic of Ireland   Greece   Singapore   France   Russia   Thailand   Argentina
South Africa   ~~Turkey~~   Mexico   New Zealand   Mongolia   China   Poland   India   Brazil
Egypt   Canada   Japan   Slovakia   Australia   Netherlands   Philippines   Portugal   Austria
South Korea   Spain   United Kingdom   Pakistan   Czech Republic
Indonesia   United Arab Emirates   Germany   United States of America   Switzerland

03 Parler de vous

Il est utile de savoir comment dire son âge et d'où l'on vient. Pour cela, vous pouvez utiliser le verbe « to be ».

⚙ **Grammaire** « To be » avec l'âge et la nationalité
Aa Vocabulaire Les nombres et les nationalités
🧩 **Compétence** Parler de vous

Aa 3.1 ÉCRIVEZ LES NOMBRES SUIVANTS EN CHIFFRES.

Three	=	3

1 Eighty-five = _____

2 Twenty-one = _____

3 Ninety = _____

4 Seventeen = _____

5 Eighty-four = _____

6 Sixty-two = _____

7 Forty-seven = _____

8 Fifty = _____

9 Seventy-one = _____

10 Twelve = _____

11 Thirty-three = _____

🔊

⚙ 3.2 RÉCRIVEZ LES PHRASES EN ÉCRIVANT LES NOMBRES EN TOUTES LETTRES.

Pamela is **42** years old.
Pamela is forty-two years old.

1 Chloe is **31** years old.

2 Heidi is **52** years old.

3 Zach is **16** years old.

4 Charlie is **10** years old.

5 Marcel is **80** years old.

6 Claire is **21** years old.

7 Dan is **36** years old.

8 Eleanor is **28** years old.

9 Rebecca is **43** years old.

🔊

3.3 UTILISEZ LE SCHÉMA POUR CRÉER 9 PHRASES, PUIS LISEZ-LES À VOIX HAUTE.

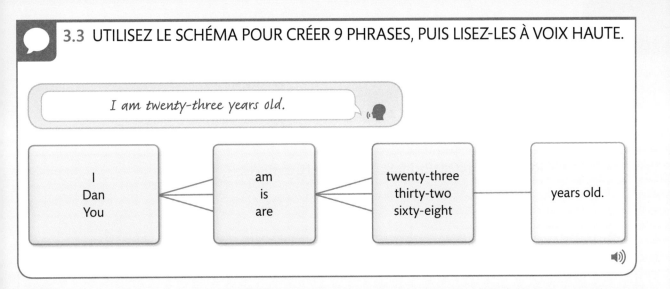

I am twenty-three years old.

I	am	twenty-three	years old.
Dan	is	thirty-two	
You	are	sixty-eight	

3.4 COMPLÉTEZ LES PHRASES AVEC LA CONJUGAISON CORRECTE DE « TO BE ».

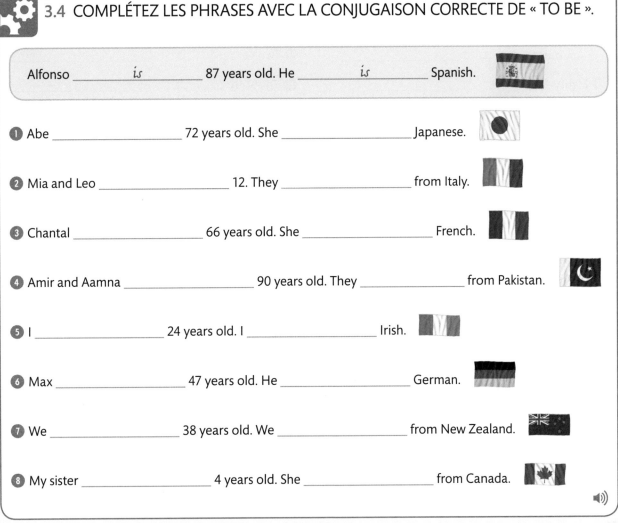

Alfonso _____*is*_____ 87 years old. He _____*is*_____ Spanish.

❶ Abe _____ 72 years old. She _____ Japanese.

❷ Mia and Leo _____ 12. They _____ from Italy.

❸ Chantal _____ 66 years old. She _____ French.

❹ Amir and Aamna _____ 90 years old. They _____ from Pakistan.

❺ I _____ 24 years old. I _____ Irish.

❻ Max _____ 47 years old. He _____ German.

❼ We _____ 38 years old. We _____ from New Zealand.

❽ My sister _____ 4 years old. She _____ from Canada.

17

Aa 4.1 LA FAMILLE DE PABLO PLACEZ LES MOTS DE LA LISTE DANS L'ARBRE GÉNÉALOGIQUE DE PABLO À L'ENDROIT CORRESPONDANT.

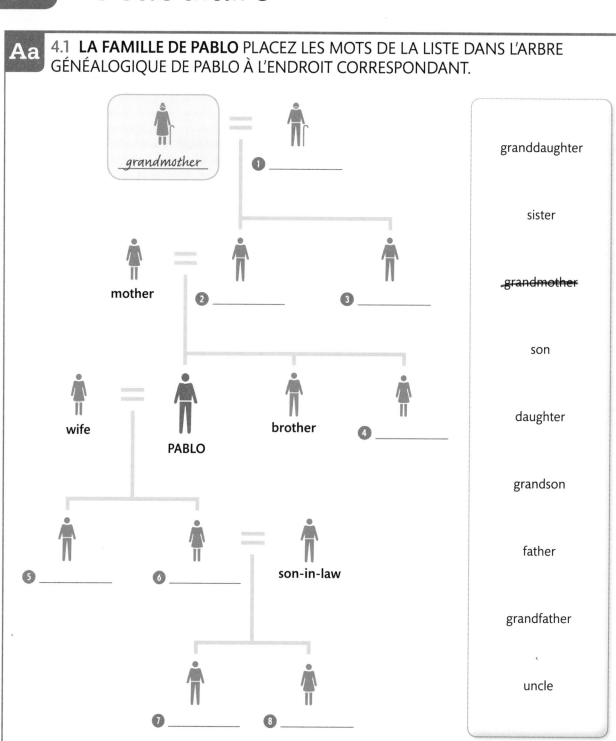

grandmother

1 _____

mother

2 _____

3 _____

wife

PABLO

brother

4 _____

5 _____

6 _____

son-in-law

7 _____

8 _____

granddaughter

sister

~~grandmother~~

son

daughter

grandson

father

grandfather

uncle

4.2 LES ANIMAUX DOMESTIQUES ET LES ANIMAUX DE LA FERME
PLACEZ LES MOTS DE LA LISTE SOUS L'ANIMAL CORRESPONDANT.

hamster

1 _____

2 _____

guinea pig

parrot

dog

chicken

snake

~~hamster~~

cat

rabbit

fish

tortoise

pig

horse

 (rabbit)

3 _____

 (tortoise)

4 _____

5 _____

6 _____

7 _____

8 _____

9 _____

10 _____

11 _____

05 Exprimer la possession

Les adjectifs possessifs permettent d'indiquer
à qui quelque chose appartient (un animal domestique
par exemple). « This » et « that » sont des déterminants.
Ils mettent l'accent sur un objet ou une personne spécifique.

⚙ **Grammaire** Les adjectifs possessifs, « this » et « that »
Aa Vocabulaire Les animaux et la famille
🧩 **Compétence** Dire à qui quelque chose appartient

 5.1 COMPLÉTEZ LES PHRASES EN UTILISANT LES ADJECTIFS POSSESSIFS APPROPRIÉS.

_____*Her*_____ (She) fish is called Nemo.

❶ _____ (They) dog is called Beth.

❷ _____ (He) tortoise is 50 years old.

❸ _____ (I) cat is called Sam.

❹ _____ (We) lion is from Kenya.

❺ _____ (You) rabbit eats grass.

❻ Here is _____ (it) bed.

❼ _____ (They) snake is called Sid.

❽ Buster is _____ (I) monkey.

❾ _____ (You) parrot is from Venezuela.

❿ _____ (She) cat is called Tabatha.

⓫ _____ (They) monkey is from Morocco.

⓬ _____ (She) pig lives on a farm.

⓭ _____ (He) horse is called Prancer.

⓮ _____ (We) chicken lives in the garden.

◀))

 5.2 RÉCRIVEZ LES PHRASES SUIVANTES EN CORRIGEANT LES ERREURS.

It is **she** horse.
It is her horse.

❶ Fido is **I** dog.
_____

❷ Cookie is **he** cat.
_____

❸ It is **we** chicken.
_____

❹ Ziggy is **you** parrot.
_____

❺ Hiss is **they** snake.
_____

❻ Max is **we** monkey.
_____

❼ It is **she** rabbit.
_____

❽ Ed is **I** horse.
_____

❾ Rex is **you** dog.
_____

❿ Nemo is **she** fish.
_____

⓫ It is **we** sheep.
_____

◀))

5.3 COMPLÉTEZ LES PHRASES AVEC « THIS » OU « THAT ».

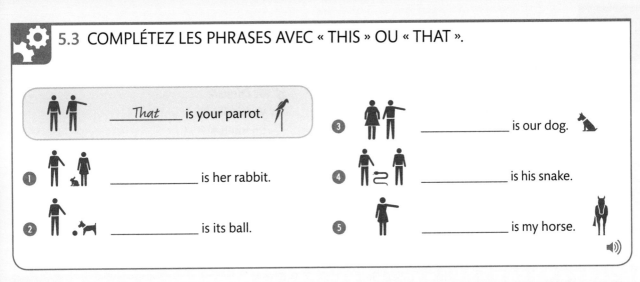

That is your parrot.

① _____ is her rabbit.

② _____ is its ball.

③ _____ is our dog.

④ _____ is his snake.

⑤ _____ is my horse.

5.4 ÉCRIVEZ LES MOTS SUIVANTS DANS LE BON ORDRE AFIN DE RECONSTITUER LES PHRASES.

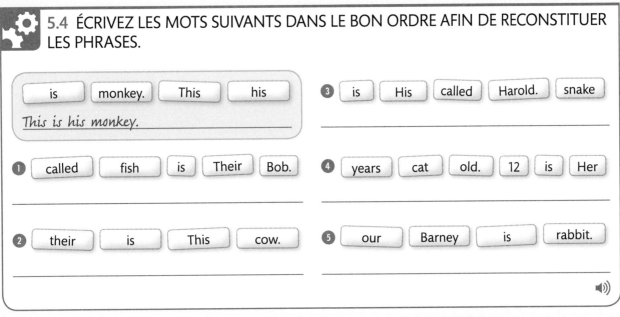

| is | monkey. | This | his |

This is his monkey.

③ | is | His | called | Harold. | snake |

_____

① | called | fish | is | Their | Bob. |

_____

④ | years | cat | old. | 12 | is | Her |

_____

② | their | is | This | cow. |

_____

⑤ | our | Barney | is | rabbit. |

_____

5.5 UTILISEZ LE SCHÉMA POUR CRÉER 12 PHRASES, PUIS LISEZ-LES À VOIX HAUTE.

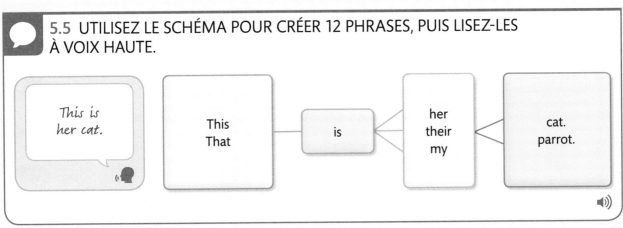

This is her cat.

| This / That | is | her / their / my | cat. / parrot. |

06 Utiliser l'apostrophe

En anglais, vous pouvez utiliser l'apostrophe (') pour indiquer la possession. Vous pouvez l'utiliser pour montrer à qui quelque chose appartient (un animal domestique, par exemple) et pour parler de votre famille.

⚙ **Grammaire** L'apostrophe possessive
Aa Vocabulaire La famille et les animaux domestiques
🧩 **Compétence** Parler de ce qui vous appartient

6.1 RÉCRIVEZ LA PHRASE EN UTILISANT UNE APOSTROPHE SUIVIE DE « S ».

The son of Christopher = *Christopher's son*

❶ The dog of Joe and Greg = _____

❷ The granddaughters of Dolly = _____

❸ The house of Sue = _____

❹ The snake of Pete and Aziz = _____

🔊

6.2 ÉCOUTEZ L'ENREGISTREMENT, PUIS RELIEZ LES PAIRES.

Angela is	Sam's mother.
❶ Arthur is	Sam's grandfather.
❷ Frank is	Sam's sister.
❸ Charlotte is	Sam's grandmother.
❹ Micky is	Sam's friend.
❺ Sally is	Sam's father.
❻ Ronaldo is	Sam's brother.
❼ Rebecca is	Sam's cousin.

6.3 LISEZ L'ARTICLE, PUIS COCHEZ LES BONNES RÉPONSES.

Sam lives with seven people.
True ☑ **False** ☐

① Esme is Sam's grandmother.
True ☐ **False** ☐

② Sam's mother is called Helen.
True ☐ **False** ☐

③ Sam's sisters go to university.
True ☐ **False** ☐

④ There are two animals in the family's home.
True ☐ **False** ☐

⑤ Ted's snake is called Bouncer.
True ☐ **False** ☐

TELEVISION

A fascinating look at everyday life with the Douglas family

Sam Douglas lives with seven other people at his home in London. Esme and Alf are Sam's grandparents. They have 14 grandchildren. Sam's mom is called Annie; she works in the pub next to the family's house. Annie's husband is Ralf and he's a mechanic.

Sam has two sisters and one brother. His sisters are called Helen and Rebecca. They go to a school near their house. Ted is Sam's brother. He's 20 and goes to university.

There are two animals in the Douglas family's home. Bouncer is Sam's dog and Hiss is Ted's snake.

6.4 RÉCRIVEZ LES PHRASES EN CORRIGEANT LES ERREURS.

This is **Rogers'** house.
This is Roger's house.

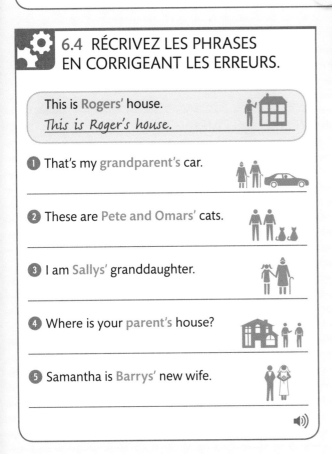

① That's my **grandparent's** car.

② These are **Pete and Omars'** cats.

③ I am **Sallys'** granddaughter.

④ Where is your **parent's** house?

⑤ Samantha is **Barrys'** new wife.

6.5 COMPLÉTEZ LES PHRASES, PUIS LISEZ-LES À VOIX HAUTE.

Sally is ____*Fred's*____ (Fred) sister.

① Sooty is _____ (my brothers) cat.

② They are _____ (Tammy) parents.

③ This is our _____ (children) snake.

④ My _____ (parents) house is small.

23

Aa 7.1 LES OBJETS DU QUOTIDIEN PLACEZ LES MOTS DE LA LISTE SOUS L'IMAGE CORRESPONDANTE.

wallet

1 _____

2 _____

3 _____

7 _____

8 _____

9 _____

10 _____

14 _____

15 _____

16 _____

17 _____

21 _____

22 _____

23 _____

24 _____

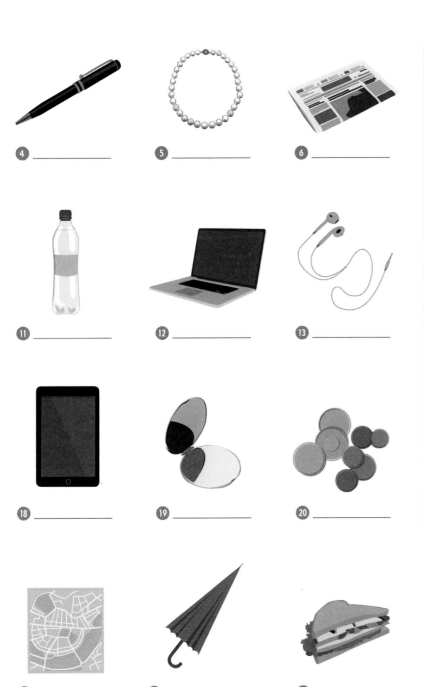

4 _____

5 _____

6 _____

11 _____

12 _____

13 _____

18 _____

19 _____

20 _____

25 _____

26 _____

27 _____

coins   dictionary

pencil   passport

camera   ID card

wallet   earphones

bottle of water   map

apple   notebook

tablet   toothbrush

sandwich   letter

mirror   sunglasses

keys   newspaper

hairbrush   necklace

book   glasses

laptop   umbrella

magazine   pen

08 Parler de ce qui vous appartient

On utilise « these » et « those » lorsque l'on parle de plusieurs choses. Pour indiquer à qui quelque chose appartient, vous pouvez utiliser des déterminants ou des pronoms possessifs.

⚙ **Grammaire** « These » et « those »
Aa Vocabulaire Vos affaires personnelles
🧩 **Compétence** Les déterminants et les pronoms

 8.1 BARREZ LE MOT INCORRECT DANS CHAQUE PHRASE.

This / ~~These~~ is my phone.

1 This / These are my mom's glasses.

2 That / Those are Samantha's keys.

3 This / These is Tom's umbrella.

4 This / These is my dog.

5 That / Those are Pete's books.

6 That / Those is your newspaper.

7 This / These are my tickets.

8 This / These are Marge's earrings.

9 This / These are his daughters.

10 That / Those is my teacher.

11 That / Those is your watch.

🔊

 8.2 RÉCRIVEZ CHAQUE PHRASE AU PLURIEL OU AU SINGULIER.

This is my sister. | These are my sisters.

1 _____ | These are my letters.

2 This is my purse. | _____

3 _____ | Those are Greg's keys.

4 That is my cat. | _____

5 _____ | These are my sister's pencils.

6 That is your dictionary. | _____

7 This is Dan's house. | _____

8 _____ | Those are Stan's books.

9 _____ | Those are my brothers.

8.3 ÉCRIVEZ LE PLURIEL DES MOTS SUIVANTS.

apple	=	*apples*	
① pencil	=	_____	
② fish	=	_____	
③ brother	=	_____	
④ diary	=	_____	
⑤ necklace	=	_____	
⑥ brush	=	_____	
⑦ watch	=	_____	
⑧ box	=	_____	
⑨ dictionary	=	_____	
⑩ sister	=	_____	
⑪ umbrella	=	_____	
⑫ laptop	=	_____	

🔊

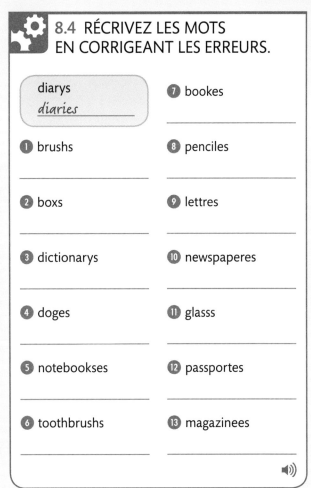

8.4 RÉCRIVEZ LES MOTS EN CORRIGEANT LES ERREURS.

diarys
diaries

① brushs
_____

② boxs
_____

③ dictionarys
_____

④ doges
_____

⑤ notebookses
_____

⑥ toothbrushs
_____

⑦ bookes
_____

⑧ penciles
_____

⑨ lettres
_____

⑩ newspaperes
_____

⑪ glasss
_____

⑫ passportes
_____

⑬ magazinees
_____

🔊

Aa 8.5 DÉCRIVEZ CHAQUE IMAGE.

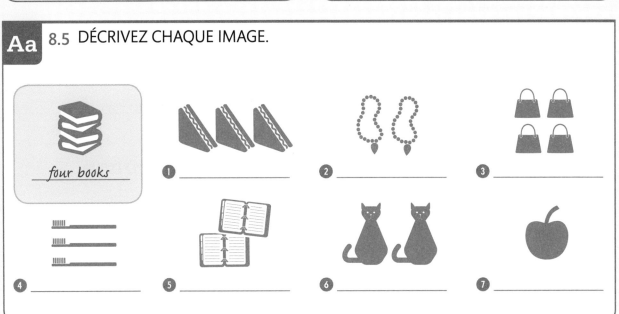

four books

① _____

② _____

③ _____

④ _____

⑤ _____

⑥ _____

⑦ _____

27

Aa 8.6 RELIEZ CHAQUE DÉTERMINANT AU PRONOM CORRESPONDANT.

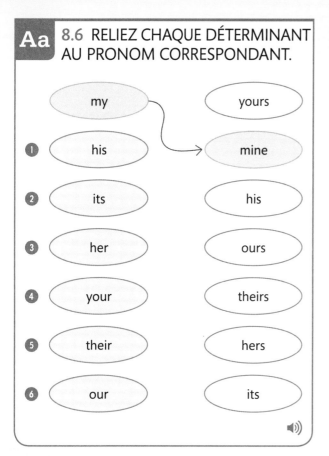

my → mine

yours

① his — mine

② its — his

③ her — ours

④ your — theirs

⑤ their — hers

⑥ our — its

🔊

8.7 REMPLACEZ LE DÉTERMINANT PAR UN PRONOM.

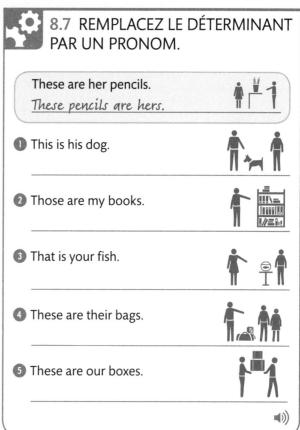

> These are her pencils.
> *These pencils are hers.*

① This is his dog.
_____

② Those are my books.
_____

③ That is your fish.
_____

④ These are their bags.
_____

⑤ These are our boxes.
_____

🔊

8.8 ÉCOUTEZ L'ENREGISTREMENT, PUIS COCHEZ LES PHRASES QUE VOUS ENTENDEZ.

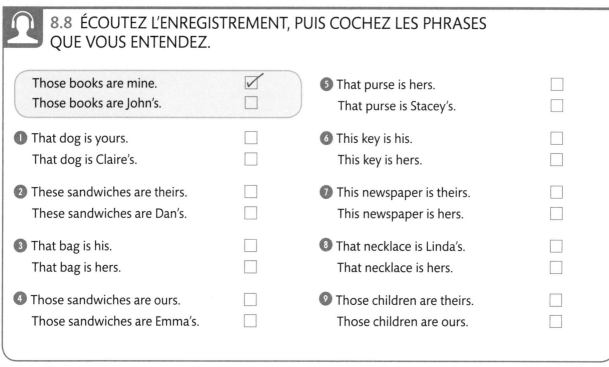

Those books are mine. ☑
Those books are John's. ☐

① That dog is yours. ☐
That dog is Claire's. ☐

② These sandwiches are theirs. ☐
These sandwiches are Dan's. ☐

③ That bag is his. ☐
That bag is hers. ☐

④ Those sandwiches are ours. ☐
Those sandwiches are Emma's. ☐

⑤ That purse is hers. ☐
That purse is Stacey's. ☐

⑥ This key is his. ☐
This key is hers. ☐

⑦ This newspaper is theirs. ☐
This newspaper is hers. ☐

⑧ That necklace is Linda's. ☐
That necklace is hers. ☐

⑨ Those children are theirs. ☐
Those children are ours. ☐

8.9 COMPLÉTEZ LES PHRASES AVEC « THIS » OU « THESE », PUIS LISEZ-LES À VOIX HAUTE.

These are my pencils.

1. _____ are my books.

2. _____ is your dog.

3. _____ are her bags.

4. _____ are their boxes.

5. _____ is my toothbrush.

6. _____ is his diary.

7. _____ is your apple.

8. _____ are my apples.

9. _____ are your glasses.

10. _____ are Kevin's keys.

11. _____ is my dad's car.

Aa 8.10 PLACEZ LES DÉTERMINANTS ET LES PRONOMS DU COURRIEL DANS L'ENCADRÉ CORRESPONDANT.

DÉTERMINANTS

_____
_____
_____

PRONOMS

_____
_____

✉   ⌄ ✕

To: Samantha

Subject: A new pet

Hi Samantha,

How are you? Thank you for your email. I have some big news: I have a new dog. His name is Rex and he is very big. I take him for a walk in the evening with my girlfriend Jane. Jane has a dog, too, but hers is very small. His name is Fido. Jane's dog likes mine!

We go to the park with our dogs every day. It's fun.

Let's meet soon,
Tim

↩ ↩↩   📎 🗑

09 Vocabulaire

scientist

1

2

3

7

8

9

10

14

15

16

17

21

22

23

24

④ _____

⑤ _____

⑥ _____

⑪ _____

⑫ _____

⑬ _____

⑱ _____

⑲ _____

⑳ _____

㉕ _____

㉖ _____

㉗ _____

cleaner   waiter

artist   electrician

businessman

mechanic   judge

sales assistant

teacher   gardener

receptionist

dentist   ~~scientist~~

construction worker

engineer   pilot

vet   fire fighter

nurse   chef

actor   hairdresser

businesswoman

doctor   farmer

police officer

waitress   driver

10 Parler de votre métier

Vous pouvez utiliser le verbe « to be » pour décrire votre métier. Le verbe « to work » (travailler) permet de fournir de plus amples informations sur votre lieu de travail et d'indiquer avec qui vous travaillez.

Grammaire Utiliser « I am » pour parler de votre métier
Aa Vocabulaire Les métiers et les lieux de travail
Compétence Décrire votre métier

10.1 RÉCRIVEZ CHAQUE PHRASE AU PLURIEL OU AU SINGULIER.

I am an actor.   *We are actors.*

① _____ They are doctors.

② You are a teacher. _____

③ _____ We are hairdressers.

④ I am a mechanic. _____

⑤ _____ You are cleaners.

⑥ She is a chef. _____

⑦ _____ They are actors.

⑧ He is a vet. _____

⑨ _____ We are police officers.

⑩ You are a farmer. _____

⑪ _____ You are waitresses.

⑫ I am a gardener. _____

⑬ _____ We are artists.

10.2 COMPLÉTEZ LES PHRASES EN UTILISANT LE VERBE ET L'ARTICLE APPROPRIÉS.

She ___*is a*___ doctor.

① I _____ actor.

② He _____ teacher.

③ He _____ chef.

④ You _____ engineer.

⑤ We _____ hairdressers.

⑥ They _____ farmers.

⑦ You _____ vet.

⑧ I _____ waiter.

⑨ She _____ nurse.

10.3 BARREZ LE MOT INCORRECT DANS CHAQUE PHRASE.

They ~~is~~ / are gardeners.

1 I am / is a vet.

2 She is / are a businesswoman.

3 We is / are doctors.

4 They is / are teachers.

5 He is / are a mechanic.

6 I am / is a driver.

7 We am / are receptionists.

8 They are / is waitresses.

9 She is / are a police officer.

10 I am / is a judge.

11 You is / are a nurse.

12 We am / are farmers.

13 She is / are a sales assistant.

14 I am / are a chef.

🔊

Aa 10.4 RELIEZ CHAQUE IMAGE AU MOT CORRESPONDANT.

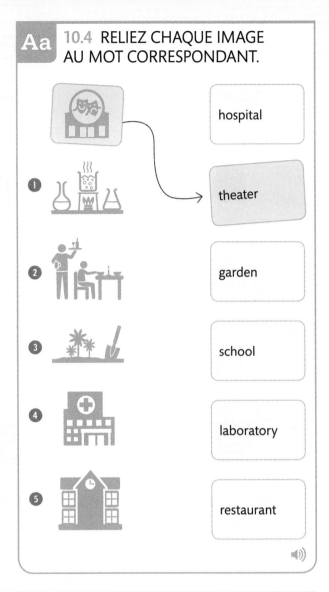

hospital

theater

garden

school

laboratory

restaurant

🔊

 10.5 BARREZ LE MOT INCORRECT DANS CHAQUE PHRASE.

I work ~~on~~ / in an office.

1 He works on / in a doctor's office.

2 We work on / in a farm.

3 My dad works on / in a building site.

4 My sister works on / in a café.

5 We work on / in people's gardens.

6 Dan works on / in a hospital.

7 I work on / in a restaurant.

8 We work on / in a school.

9 Chris works on / in a supermarket.

🔊

10.6 OBSERVEZ LES IMAGES, COMPLÉTEZ LES PHRASES AVEC LES MOTS DE LA LISTE, PUIS LISEZ-LES À VOIX HAUTE.

Eric _____*is a waiter.*_____
He _*works in a restaurant.*_

1

Abby _____
She _____

2

Julie _____
She _____

3

Simon _____
He _____

4

Adam _____
He _____

5

Max _____
He _____

6

Carol _____
She _____

~~waiter~~   police officer   park   nurse

hairdresser   ~~restaurant~~   engineer

police station   hospital

beauty salon   gardener   farm

construction site   farmer

Aa 10.7 EN VOUS AIDANT DES IMAGES, COMPLÉTEZ LES PHRASES AVEC LES MOTS DE LA LISTE.

Peter is a ___teacher___ ( ) and he works with ___children___ ( ).

1. Sam is a _____ ( ) and she works with _____ ( ).

2. Gabriella is a _____ ( ) and she works with _____ ( ).

3. Dan is a _____ ( ) and he works with _____ ( ).

4. John is a _____ ( ) and he works with _____ ( ).

5. Tom is an _____ ( ) and he works in a _____ ( ).

doctor	crops	theater	patients	chef	~~children~~
~~teacher~~	animals	food	vet	farmer	actor

10.8 ÉCOUTEZ L'ENREGISTREMENT, PUIS COCHEZ LA BONNE RÉPONSE.

Pete is a...
farmer. ✓ contractor. ☐ gardener. ☐

1. Simon is a...
contractor. ☐ gardener. ☐ teacher. ☐

2. Sue is a...
nurse. ☐ chef. ☐ teacher. ☐

3. John is a...
scientist. ☐ businessman. ☐ doctor. ☐

4. Alberto is a...
waiter. ☐ chef. ☐ actor. ☐

5. Susan and Pam are...
chefs. ☐ hairdressers. ☐ gardeners. ☐

6. Douglas is an...
actor. ☐ farmer. ☐ police officer. ☐

7. Danny is a...
contractor. ☐ architect. ☐ farmer. ☐

11 Dire l'heure

Il existe 2 manières de dire l'heure en anglais.
Vous pouvez utiliser les heures et les minutes,
ou dire les minutes en premier et préciser ensuite
leur relation à l'heure.

⚙ **Grammaire** L'heure
Aa Vocabulaire Le vocabulaire du temps
🧩 **Compétence** Dire l'heure qu'il est

Aa 11.1 RELIEZ CHAQUE HORLOGE À L'HEURE CORRESPONDANTE.

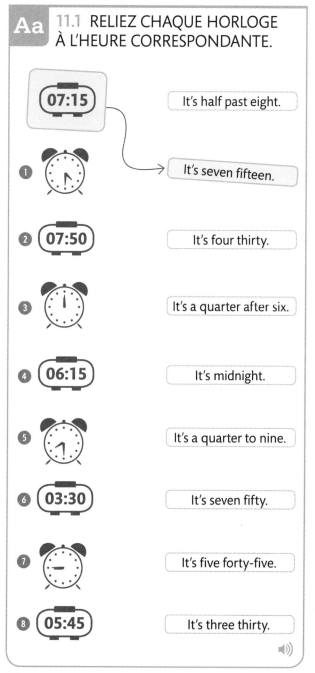

07:15

It's half past eight.

① → It's seven fifteen.

② 07:50

It's four thirty.

③ It's a quarter after six.

④ 06:15 It's midnight.

⑤ It's a quarter to nine.

⑥ 03:30 It's seven fifty.

⑦ It's five forty-five.

⑧ 05:45 It's three thirty.

🎧 11.2 ÉCOUTEZ L'ENREGISTREMENT, PUIS COCHEZ CE QUE VOUS ENTENDEZ.

05:45 ☑ | 06:15 ☐ ⑦ 03:35 ☐ | 03:25 ☐

① 07:45 ☐ | 08:15 ☐ ⑧ 09:45 ☐ | 10:45 ☐

② 07:30 ☐ | 08:30 ☐ ⑨ 06:38 ☐ | 06:28 ☐

③ 11:15 ☐ | 10:45 ☐ ⑩ 05:05 ☐ | 05:30 ☐

④ 09:30 ☐ | 09:20 ☐ ⑪ 10:00 ☐ | 10:10 ☐

⑤ 11:00 ☐ | 10:00 ☐ ⑫ 02:13 ☐ | 02:30 ☐

⑥ 07:45 ☐ | 07:15 ☐ ⑬ 08:15 ☐ | 07:45 ☐

RÉCRIVEZ LES PHRASES EN CHIFFRES.

It's a quarter to six. = 05:45

1 It's a quarter past eleven. = _____

2 It's eleven o'clock. = _____

3 It's eight twenty-four. = _____

4 It's half past three. = _____

5 It's a quarter to three. = _____

6 It's five twenty-five. = _____

7 It's three forty-nine. = _____

8 It's two fifteen. = _____

9 It's nine o'clock. = _____

10 It's a quarter to eight. = _____

11 It's half past eleven. = _____

12 It's nine twenty-five. = _____

13 It's a quarter after ten. = _____

14 It's eleven twenty. = _____

15 It's one fifty-five. = _____

16 It's quarter to seven. = _____

17 It's six forty-five. = _____

11.4 OBSERVEZ CHAQUE HORLOGE, ÉCRIVEZ L'HEURE CORRESPONDANTE, PUIS LISEZ-LES À VOIX HAUTE.

09:15 — It's a quarter past nine.

1 09:45 — _____

2 04:00 — _____

3 10:20 — _____

4 11:30 — _____

5 03:47 — _____

6 03:15 — _____

7 06:30 — _____

8 08:22 — _____

9 01:25 — _____

12 Vocabulaire

12.1 LES ROUTINES QUOTIDIENNES PLACEZ LES MOTS DE LA LISTE SOUS L'IMAGE CORRESPONDANTE.

go to work

1 _____

2 _____

3 _____

7 _____

8 _____

9 _____

10 _____

14 _____

15 _____

16 _____

17 _____

21 _____

22 _____

23 _____

24 _____

4 _____

5 _____

6 _____

11 _____

12 _____

13 _____

18 _____

19 _____

20 _____

25 _____

26 _____

27 _____

start work   clear the table

wash your face   wake up

go to bed   cook dinner

~~go to work~~   iron a shirt

leave work   get dressed

do the dishes   have dinner

go to school   walk the dog

buy groceries   take a shower

dawn   have lunch   get up

brush your teeth   go home

day   finish work   dusk

brush your hair   take a bath

have breakfast   night

13 Décrire votre journée

Utilisez le présent simple pour parler de choses que vous faites régulièrement : par exemple, l'heure à laquelle vous allez travailler ou manger.

 Grammaire Le présent simple
Aa Vocabulaire Les actions de la routine quotidienne
Compétence Parler de votre routine quotidienne

Aa 13.1 RELIEZ L'IMAGE À LA PHRASE CORRESPONDANTE.

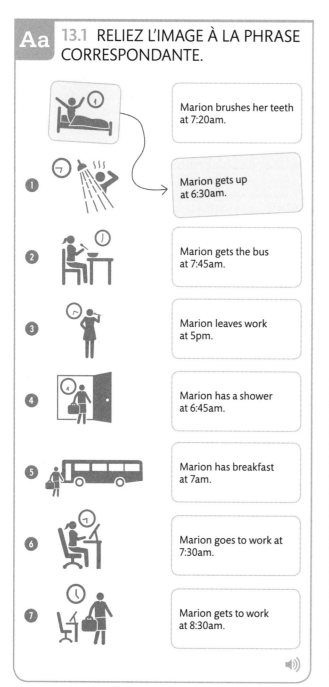

Marion brushes her teeth at 7:20am.

Marion gets up at 6:30am.

Marion gets the bus at 7:45am.

Marion leaves work at 5pm.

Marion has a shower at 6:45am.

Marion has breakfast at 7am.

Marion goes to work at 7:30am.

Marion gets to work at 8:30am.

13.2 BARREZ LE MOT INCORRECT DANS CHAQUE PHRASE.

She eats / ~~eat~~ dinner in the evening.

1 I **wake** / **wakes** up at 6:30am.

2 He **gets** / **get** up at 6am.

3 She **have** / **has** a shower at 7am.

4 They **have** / **has** cereal for breakfast.

5 He **have** / **has** a shower before breakfast.

6 She **leaves** / **leave** home at 7:15am.

7 The bus **go** / **goes** every half hour.

8 I **get** / **gets** to work at 8:30am.

9 He **start** / **starts** work at 9am.

10 She **take** / **takes** an hour for lunch.

11 I **go** / **goes** to the sandwich shop for lunch.

12 They **eat** / **eats** lunch in the canteen.

13 He **finish** / **finishes** work at 5pm.

14 They **go** / **goes** home on the bus.

15 He **wash** / **washes** his car every weekend.

16 I **watch** / **watches** TV after dinner.

17 They **go** / **goes** to bed at 11pm.

18 He **sleep** / **sleeps** for eight hours.

13.3 COMPLÉTEZ LES PHRASES EN CONJUGUANT LES VERBES À LA BONNE FORME.

I eat   =   She _____*eats*_____

1. I have   =   He _____
2. I start   =   It _____
3. I leave   =   He _____
4. I get up   =   She _____

5. I go   =   It _____
6. I wake up   =   She _____
7. I wash   =   He _____
8. I watch   =   She _____
9. I finish   =   It _____

13.4 COMPLÉTEZ LES PHRASES EN CONJUGUANT LES VERBES À LA BONNE FORME.

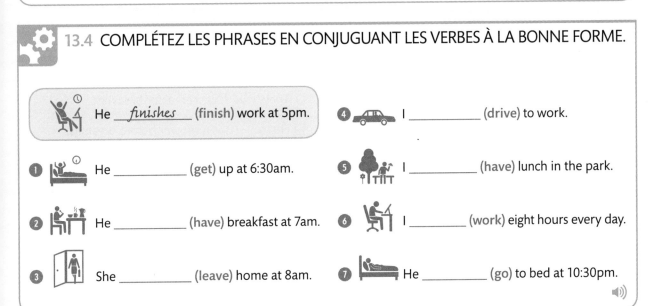

He _____*finishes*_____ (finish) work at 5pm.

1. He _____ (get) up at 6:30am.
2. He _____ (have) breakfast at 7am.
3. She _____ (leave) home at 8am.

4. I _____ (drive) to work.
5. I _____ (have) lunch in the park.
6. I _____ (work) eight hours every day.
7. He _____ (go) to bed at 10:30pm.

13.5 LISEZ CES VERBES À VOIX HAUTE.

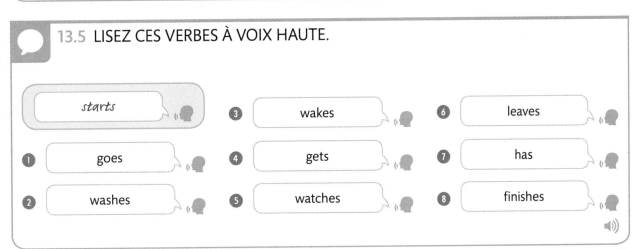

starts

1. goes
2. washes
3. wakes
4. gets
5. watches
6. leaves
7. has
8. finishes

14 Décrire votre semaine

Vous pouvez parler de vos activités hebdomadaires habituelles en utilisant le présent simple et des expressions de temps. Celles-ci sont généralement formées avec des prépositions et des jours de la semaine.

☼ Grammaire Les jours et les prépositions
Aa Vocabulaire Les jours de la semaine
🧩 Compétence Parler de votre routine hebdomadaire

14.1 COMPLÉTEZ LES PHRASES AVEC « ON » OU « IN ».

Peter plays soccer __on__ Sundays.

1 I go to the movies _____ the weekend.

2 Joe starts work at 6pm _____ Mondays.

3 You watch TV _____ the afternoon.

4 Harry plays tennis _____ Wednesdays.

5 Lin goes swimming _____ the evening.

6 Alex goes fishing _____ the weekend.

7 He eats lunch at 1pm _____ Fridays.

8 Sam goes to the gym _____ the morning.

🔊

14.2 COCHEZ LA PHRASE CORRECTE.

I play soccer on Mondays. ☑
I play soccer at Mondays. ☐

1 I work from Monday to Thursday. ☐
I work of Monday to Thursday. ☐

2 My sister go swimming every day. ☐
My sister goes swimming every day. ☐

3 We go to the gym on Saturdays. ☐
We go to the gym at Saturdays. ☐

4 You read the newspaper in Sundays. ☐
You read the newspaper on Sundays. ☐

5 Peter goes to work on the weekend. ☐
Peter goes to work from the weekend. ☐

6 Jennifer goes to a café for Fridays. ☐
Jennifer goes to a café on Fridays. ☐

7 Sam and Pete work to 9am from 5pm. ☐
Sam and Pete work from 9am to 5pm. ☐

🔊

14.3 COMPLÉTEZ LES PHRASES, PUIS LISEZ-LES À VOIX HAUTE.

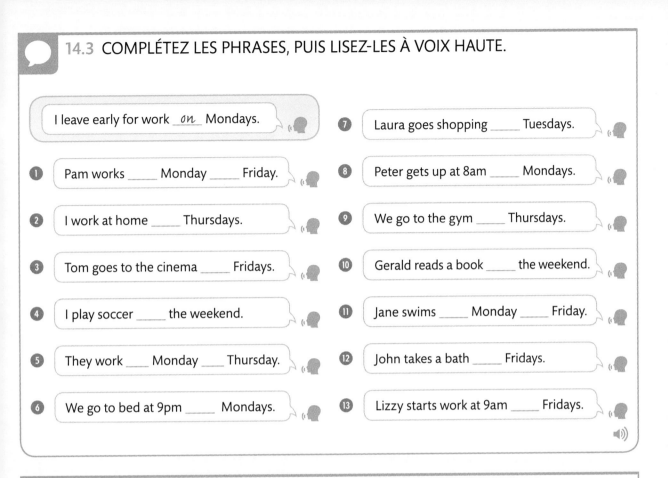

I leave early for work _on_ Mondays.

7 Laura goes shopping _____ Tuesdays.

1 Pam works _____ Monday _____ Friday.

8 Peter gets up at 8am _____ Mondays.

2 I work at home _____ Thursdays.

9 We go to the gym _____ Thursdays.

3 Tom goes to the cinema _____ Fridays.

10 Gerald reads a book _____ the weekend.

4 I play soccer _____ the weekend.

11 Jane swims _____ Monday _____ Friday.

5 They work _____ Monday _____ Thursday.

12 John takes a bath _____ Fridays.

6 We go to bed at 9pm _____ Mondays.

13 Lizzy starts work at 9am _____ Fridays.

14.4 ÉCRIVEZ LES MOTS SUIVANTS DANS LE BON ORDRE AFIN DE RECONSTITUER LES PHRASES.

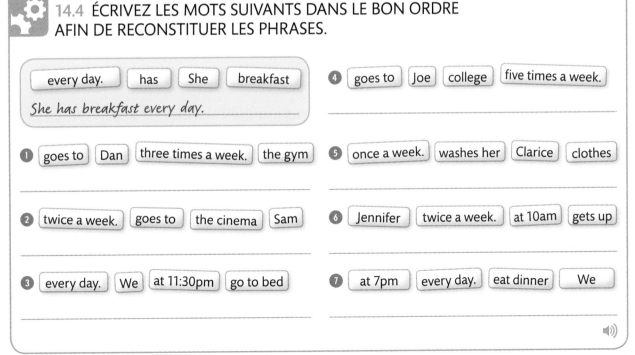

every day.　has　She　breakfast

She has breakfast every day.

4 goes to　Joe　college　five times a week.

_____

1 goes to　Dan　three times a week.　the gym

_____

5 once a week.　washes her　Clarice　clothes

_____

2 twice a week.　goes to　the cinema　Sam

_____

6 Jennifer　twice a week.　at 10am　gets up

_____

3 every day.　We　at 11:30pm　go to bed

_____

7 at 7pm　every day.　eat dinner　We

_____

14.5 RÉCRIVEZ LES PHRASES SUIVANTES EN CORRIGEANT LES ERREURS.

> I wakes up at 6:30am.
> *I wake up at 6:30am.*

1 Bob go swimming on Thursdays.

2 I play tennis on weekend.

3 Jane and Tom go to the gym three time a week.

4 Angus works from Monday on Thursday.

5 I go to the movies on weekend.

6 Sam goes to college Wednesdays.

7 Jenny gets up in 7am every day.

8 Peter work from Monday to Friday.

9 Nina go to bed at 11pm every day.

14.6 LISEZ LE COURRIEL, PUIS COCHEZ LES BONNES RÉPONSES.

> Jim goes to the gym three times a week.
> **True** ☐ **False** ☑

1 Jim goes to work at 6am.
True ☐ **False** ☐

2 Jim goes to the gym on Mondays and Tuesdays.
True ☐ **False** ☐

3 He plays soccer on Fridays.
True ☐ **False** ☐

4 Jim and his wife get up at 10am on the weekend.
True ☐ **False** ☐

5 They go to the theater on Saturdays.
True ☐ **False** ☐

6 They go to a restaurant on Sundays.
True ☐ **False** ☐

✉

To: Pete

Subject: My week

Hi Pete,
Let me tell you about my typical week. From Monday to Thursday, I get up early, at 6am. I eat breakfast, then I go to work at 8:30am. On Fridays, I work at home. I like Fridays. I like sports a lot. I go to the gym twice a week, on Mondays and Tuesdays, and I go swimming on Wednesdays. I play soccer on Thursdays, but I relax on Friday and read a newspaper.

On the weekend, my wife and I get up at 10am. We go to the movies on Saturdays, and on Sundays, we go to a good restaurant. Tell me about your weekend!

Jim

14.7 ÉCOUTEZ L'ENREGISTREMENT, PUIS NUMÉROTEZ LES IMAGES DANS LE BON ORDRE.

A ☐

B ☐

C ☐

D ☐

E 1

F ☐

14.8 RÉÉCOUTEZ L'ENREGISTREMENT DE L'EXERCICE 14.7, PUIS COCHEZ LES BONNES RÉPONSES.

Kate goes to the gym on...
Monday ☐ **Tuesday** ☐ **Friday** ✓

❶ Paul is a...
farmer ☐ **teacher** ☐ **doctor** ☐

❷ Jane is a...
nurse ☐ **doctor** ☐ **teacher** ☐

❸ On the weekend, Jane goes to...
a restaurant ☐ **the movies** ☐ **a gym** ☐

❹ Sally gets up at...
6am ☐ **7am** ☐ **8am** ☐

❺ Sally goes swimming on...
Saturday ☐ **Sunday** ☐ **Thursday** ☐

❻ Eric works at the...
school ☐ **theater** ☐ **restaurant** ☐

❼ Eric works... a week.
twice ☐ **three days** ☐ **four days** ☐

❽ Claire is a...
waitress ☐ **carpenter** ☐ **farmer** ☐

❾ Claire starts work at...
6am ☐ **4pm** ☐ **6pm** ☐

15 « To be » à la forme négative

Pour former une phrase négative, vous devez utiliser « not » ou sa forme contractée « n't ». Les règles pour les phrases négatives avec le verbe « to be » sont différentes de celles pour les phrases négatives avec d'autres verbes.

⚙ **Grammaire** « To be » à la forme négative

Aa Vocabulaire « Not »

🧩 **Compétence** Dire ce que les choses ne sont pas

15.1 ÉCRIVEZ LES MOTS DANS LE BON ORDRE AFIN DE RECONSTITUER LES PHRASES.

o'clock. | 5 | not | is | It

It is not 5 o'clock.

① teacher. | Paula | not | is | a

② are | not | England. | We | from

③ my | This | phone. | not | is

④ years | Kirsty | not | old. | 18 | is

⑤ is | not | Frank | my | father.

⑥ This | my | not | purse. | is

⑦ not | They | are | engineers.

⑧ is | That | salon. | not | a

⑨ Kim | a | teacher. | is | not

🔊

15.2 COMPLÉTEZ EN FORMANT DES PHRASES NÉGATIVES.

They _____*are not*_____ hairdressers.

① That _____ a castle.

② They _____ at school.

③ He _____ a grandfather.

④ We _____ engineers.

⑤ She _____ 70 years old.

⑥ You _____ French.

⑦ This _____ my dog.

⑧ I _____ a doctor.

⑨ It _____ 11 o'clock.

🔊

46

15.3 ÉCOUTEZ L'ENREGISTREMENT, PUIS NUMÉROTEZ LES IMAGES DANS LE BON ORDRE.

 A ☐

 B 1

 C ☐

 D ☐

15.4 RÉCRIVEZ CHAQUE PHRASE DE 2 MANIÈRES DIFFÉRENTES.

She is not a nurse.	*She's not a nurse.*	*She isn't a nurse.*
1	Fredo's not a chef.	
2 Susie is not my cat.		
3		My dad isn't at work.
4	They're not at the theater.	

15.5 LISEZ LE BLOG, PUIS COCHEZ LES BONNES RÉPONSES.

Mia is 45 years old.	True ☐ False ☑
1 She lives in California.	True ☐ False ☐
2 She's a waitress in a restaurant.	True ☐ False ☐
3 She isn't Mexican.	True ☐ False ☐
4 Franco isn't an engineer.	True ☐ False ☐
5 They have a daughter in college.	True ☐ False ☐

Mia's blog

HOME | ENTRIES | ABOUT | CONTACT

POSTED MONDAY, APRIL 20

My life

Hi! I'm Mia and I'm 47 years old. I live in Los Angeles, California, and I'm a chef. I work in a Mexican restaurant. A lot of people think I'm from Mexico, but I'm not. I'm from Colombia. I'm married to Franco. He's a carpenter. We have a son, Sam. He studies at a local college.

15.6 RÉCRIVEZ LES PHRASES SUIVANTES EN CORRIGEANT LES ERREURS.

This **aren't** your cat.
This isn't your cat.

1 This **aren't** his umbrella.

2 Pedro **aren't** Spanish.

3 Pete and Terry **isn't** hairdressers.

4 It **aren't** a snake.

5 My cousins **isn't** 21 years old.

6 It **aren't** half past six.

7 I **isn't** your friend.

15.7 LISEZ LE BLOG, PUIS COCHEZ LES BONNES RÉPONSES.

Theresa is not from Germany.
True ☐ **False** ☑

1 Lucia is not 41 years old.
True ☐ **False** ☐

2 There isn't a learner from Spain.
True ☐ **False** ☐

3 Pablo is not a teacher.
True ☐ **False** ☐

4 Theresa is not a teacher.
True ☐ **False** ☐

5 Xi is not a chef.
True ☐ **False** ☐

6 Xi does not live in China.
True ☐ **False** ☐

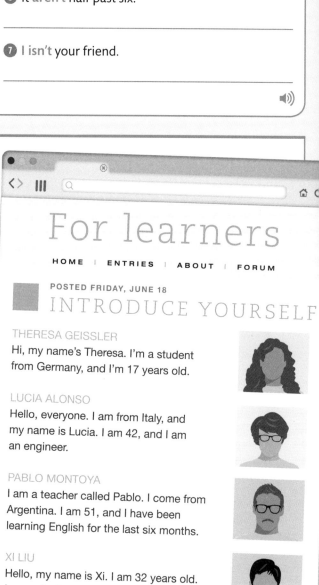

For learners

HOME | ENTRIES | ABOUT | FORUM

POSTED FRIDAY, JUNE 18
INTRODUCE YOURSELF

THERESA GEISSLER
Hi, my name's Theresa. I'm a student from Germany, and I'm 17 years old.

LUCIA ALONSO
Hello, everyone. I am from Italy, and my name is Lucia. I am 42, and I am an engineer.

PABLO MONTOYA
I am a teacher called Pablo. I come from Argentina. I am 51, and I have been learning English for the last six months.

XI LIU
Hello, my name is Xi. I am 32 years old. I am a doctor, and I live with my wife and son in China.

15.8 REMPLACEZ « YOU » PAR « I » DANS LES PHRASES.

> You're a nurse. You're not a doctor.
> *I'm a nurse. I'm not a doctor.*

1 You're a student. You're not a teacher.

2 You're 30 years old. You're not 40.

3 You're a farmer. You're not a police officer.

4 You're French. You're not English.

5 You're an uncle. You're not a father.

6 You're 18. You're not 21.

7 You're a waitress. You're not a chef.

8 You're Spanish. You're not Italian.

 15.9 REMPLACEZ « I » PAR « YOU » DANS LES PHRASES.

> I'm French. I'm not German.
> *You're French. You're not German.*

1 I'm 28. I'm not 29.

2 I'm a scientist. I'm not a gardener.

3 I'm Austrian. I'm not English.

4 I'm a contractor. I'm not an actor.

5 I'm 16. I'm not 18.

6 I'm an uncle. I'm not a grandfather.

7 I'm a mechanic. I'm not an engineer.

8 I'm a police officer. I'm not a firefighter.

 15.10 UTILISEZ LE SCHÉMA POUR CRÉER 12 PHRASES, PUIS LISEZ-LES À VOIX HAUTE.

> *I'm not at work.*

| I You She | 'm not isn't aren't | at work. an actor. American. 40 years old. |

16 Les autres négations

Pour mettre le présent à la forme négative, il suffit d'ajouter « do not » ou « does not » devant la plupart des verbes. Ces formes sont souvent contractées en « don't » ou « doesn't ».

⚙ **Grammaire** Le présent simple à la forme négative
Aa Vocabulaire Les activités quotidiennes
🧩 **Compétence** Dire ce que vous ne faites pas

⚙ 16.1 COMPLÉTEZ LES PHRASES AVEC « DO NOT » OU « DOES NOT ».

She __*does not*__ play tennis on Wednesdays.

1 Jane _____ walk to work.

2 My brother _____ watch TV.

3 I _____ read a book in the evening.

4 Frank _____ work at the museum.

5 They _____ go dancing on the weekend.

6 We _____ go to work on Fridays.

7 I _____ get up at 7:30am.

8 You _____ have a car.

9 My dad _____ work in an office.

10 You _____ have a dog.

11 My sister _____ work with children.

12 They _____ live in the country.

13 Freddie _____ eat meat.

🔊

⚙ 16.2 ÉCRIVEZ LES MOTS SUIVANTS DANS LE BON ORDRE AFIN DE RECONSTITUER LES PHRASES.

[go] [Mick] [on Wednesdays.] [to work] [doesn't]

Mick doesn't go to work on Wednesdays.

1 [in New York.] [live] [doesn't] [Tony]

_____

2 [doesn't] [a farm.] [work] [on] [Sebastian]

_____

3 [a factory.] [doesn't] [uncle] [My] [in] [work]

_____

4 [on Thursdays.] [soccer] [play] [We] [don't]

_____

5 [German] [don't] [at school.] [I] [learn]

_____

6 [work] [Carlo] [on Mondays.] [doesn't]

_____

7 [don't] [at] [You] [take] [a bath] [night.]

_____

🔊

16.3 RÉCRIVEZ LES PHRASES EN UTILISANT 2 FORMES NÉGATIVES DIFFÉRENTES.

I get up at 7am.	I do not get up at 7am.	I don't get up at 7am.
1 Tim plays tennis.		
2 You have a black cat.		
3 Jules reads a book every day.		
4 Sam works in a restaurant.		
5 They play soccer.		
6 Emily works with animals.		
7 Mel and Greg have a car.		
8 You work in a factory.		

 16.4 RÉCRIVEZ LES PHRASES EN CORRIGEANT LES ERREURS.

He don't go swimming on Wednesdays.
He doesn't go swimming on Wednesdays.

1 Chloe don't play tennis with her friends.

_____

2 You doesn't work outside.

_____

3 Sal and Doug doesn't have a car.

_____

4 We doesn't watch TV at home.

_____

5 Mrs. O'Brien don't work in an office.

_____

6 You doesn't wake up at 6am.

_____

7 They doesn't eat lunch at 1pm.

_____

8 Virginia don't speak good English.

_____

9 Trevor don't live near here.

_____

10 My dad don't live in Los Angeles.

_____

11 David don't play chess.

_____

Aa 16.5 ÉCOUTEZ L'ENREGISTREMENT, PUIS COCHEZ LES BONNES RÉPONSES.

Jenny doesn't work in a bank. ☑
Jenny don't work in a bank. ☐

1 Jean don't cycle to work. ☐
Jean doesn't cycle to work. ☐

2 They don't live in the city. ☐
They doesn't live in the city. ☐

3 Mr. James don't go to the theater. ☐
Mr. James doesn't go to the theater. ☐

4 He doesn't read a newspaper. ☐
He don't read a newspaper. ☐

5 My cousins don't have tickets. ☐
My cousins doesn't have tickets. ☐

6 Sally doesn't go to the gym. ☐
Sally don't go to the gym. ☐

7 Our dog don't have a ball. ☐
Our dog doesn't have a ball. ☐

8 I don't have a laptop. ☐
I doesn't have a laptop. ☐

9 My mom doesn't get up at 7:30am. ☐
My mom don't get up at 7:30am. ☐

10 You doesn't live in the country. ☐
You don't live in the country. ☐

11 Claude don't have a dictionary. ☐
Claude doesn't have a dictionary. ☐

16.6 ÉCOUTEZ L'ENREGISTREMENT, PUIS COCHEZ LES BONNES RÉPONSES.

Julie décrit sa semaine.

Julie works in the museum.
True ☑ False ☐

1 Julie gets up at 7am.
True ☐ False ☐

2 Julie doesn't work on Fridays.
True ☐ False ☐

3 Julie has lunch with her friends.
True ☐ False ☐

4 Julie plays tennis on Wednesday evenings.
True ☐ False ☐

5 Julie gets home at 8pm.
True ☐ False ☐

6 Julie doesn't eat dinner.
True ☐ False ☐

7 Julie watches TV before she goes to bed.
True ☐ False ☐

16.7 LISEZ L'ARTICLE SUIVANT, PUIS COCHEZ LES BONNES RÉPONSES.

Who doesn't live in a city?
Sam ☐ **Carla** ☐ **Greg** ☑

❶ Who plays a sport on Thursdays?
Sam ☐ **Carla** ☐ **Greg** ☐

❷ Who works in the evenings?
Sam ☐ **Carla** ☐ **Greg** ☐

❸ Who doesn't have lunch?
Sam ☐ **Carla** ☐ **Greg** ☐

❹ Who works in an office?
Sam ☐ **Carla** ☐ **Greg** ☐

❺ Who doesn't work on Mondays?
Sam ☐ **Carla** ☐ **Greg** ☐

❻ Who starts work at 5am?
Sam ☐ **Carla** ☐ **Greg** ☐

❼ Who plays basketball on Mondays?
Sam ☐ **Carla** ☐ **Greg** ☐

❽ Who plays soccer?
Sam ☐ **Carla** ☐ **Greg** ☐

What I do

Sam

I'm a waiter from New York. I like my job. I work evenings and the food is fantastic. I work from Tuesday to Sunday, and I don't work on Mondays. On Mondays I play basketball in the afternoon.

Carla

I work in an office in Dublin. I start work at 9am and have lunch at 1pm. I love sports. I play soccer with my colleagues on Thursday evenings.

Greg

I live in the country in South Australia. I work on a farm and start work at 5am. I have a big breakfast and a big dinner, but I don't have lunch. Every weekend, I play golf.

16.8 UTILISEZ LE SCHÉMA POUR CRÉER 9 PHRASES, PUIS LISEZ-LES À VOIX HAUTE.

I don't go swimming.

| I / Frank / We | don't / doesn't | go swimming. / have a car. / speak Japanese. |

17 Les questions simples

Pour poser des questions simples avec le verbe
« to be », il suffit de changer l'ordre du sujet et du verbe.
La réponse à une question simple commence
généralement par « yes » ou « no ».

⚙ **Grammaire** Les questions simples
Aa Vocabulaire Les métiers et les activités de routine
🧩 **Compétence** Poser des questions simples

17.1 RÉCRIVEZ LES PHRASES SUIVANTES À LA FORME INTERROGATIVE.

She is an engineer.
Is she an engineer?

❶ This is his passport.

❷ It is 6 o'clock.

❸ Doug and Jim are hairdressers.

❹ These are my glasses.

❺ Sally is his sister.

❻ Those are your letters.

❼ She is a nurse.

❽ This is your snake.

❾ It is 3pm.

❿ His wife is a chef.

⓫ Katie and Jess are my friends.

17.2 UTILISEZ LE SCHÉMA POUR CRÉER 6 PHRASES, PUIS LISEZ-LES À VOIX HAUTE.

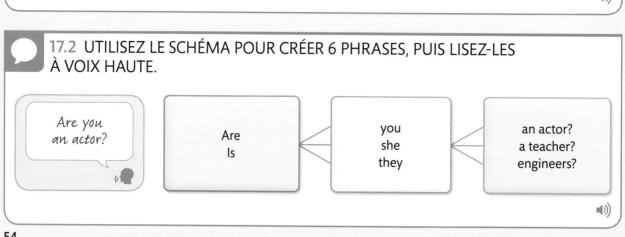

Are you an actor?

Are	you	an actor?
Is	she	a teacher?
	they	engineers?

17.3 COMPLÉTEZ LES PHRASES AVEC « IS » OU « ARE ».

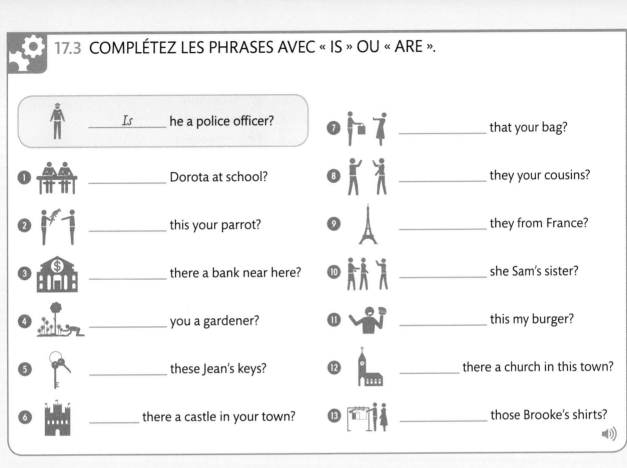

_Is_ _____ he a police officer?

1. _____ Dorota at school?

2. _____ this your parrot?

3. _____ there a bank near here?

4. _____ you a gardener?

5. _____ these Jean's keys?

6. _____ there a castle in your town?

7. _____ that your bag?

8. _____ they your cousins?

9. _____ they from France?

10. _____ she Sam's sister?

11. _____ this my burger?

12. _____ there a church in this town?

13. _____ those Brooke's shirts?

17.4 ÉCRIVEZ LES MOTS SUIVANTS DANS LE BON ORDRE AFIN DE RECONSTITUER LES PHRASES.

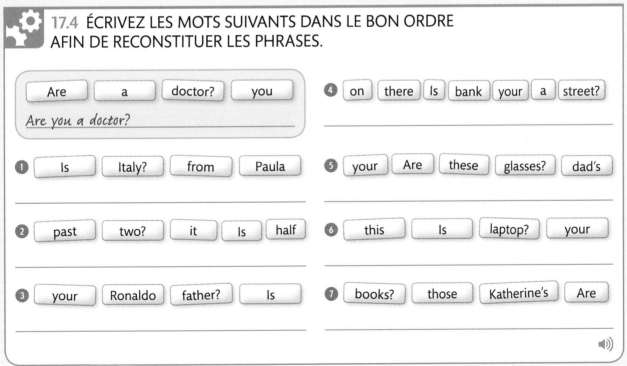

| Are | a | doctor? | you |

Are you a doctor?

1. | Is | Italy? | from | Paula |

2. | past | two? | it | Is | half |

3. | your | Ronaldo | father? | Is |

4. | on | there | Is | bank | your | a | street? |

5. | your | Are | these | glasses? | dad's |

6. | this | Is | laptop? | your |

7. | books? | those | Katherine's | Are |

17.5 COMPLÉTEZ LES PHRASES AVEC « DO » OU « DOES ».

 Does Maria go swimming?

1 _____ you work in a hospital?

2 _____ your dog like children?

3 _____ you get up at 10am on Sundays?

4 _____ Simone work with children?

5 _____ they live in the town?

6 _____ we finish work at 3pm today?

7 _____ Frank play tennis with Pete?

17.6 BARREZ LE MOT INCORRECT DANS CHAQUE QUESTION.

Do / ~~Does~~ they play tennis together?

1 Do / Does you read a newspaper every day?

2 Do / Does he go to bed at 11pm?

3 Do / Does they live in a castle?

4 Do / Does Pedro come from Bolivia?

5 Do / Does she work with children?

6 Do / Does Claire and Sam eat lunch at 2pm?

7 Do / Does your brother work with animals?

8 Do / Does Tim play soccer on Mondays?

9 Do / Does they work in a café?

10 Do / Does you have a shower in the evening?

11 Do / Does we start work at 10am on Thursdays?

12 Do / Does Pamela work in a bank?

17.7 RÉCRIVEZ CHAQUE PHRASE À LA FORME INTERROGATIVE.

Bill gets up at 7am.
Does Bill get up at 7am?

1 They work in a museum.

_____

2 You work with children.

_____

3 Shane lives in Sydney.

_____

4 John plays tennis on Wednesdays.

_____

5 Yves and Marie eat dinner at 6pm.

_____

6 Seth works in a post office.

_____

17.8 LISEZ LE COURRIEL, PUIS COCHEZ LES BONNES RÉPONSES.

Does Sam get up at 7:30am?
Yes ☐ No ☑

1 Does Sam have a bath?
Yes ☐ No ☐

2 Does he eat breakfast at home?
Yes ☐ No ☐

3 Does he eat some fruit at work?
Yes ☐ No ☐

4 Does he work in a bank?
Yes ☐ No ☐

5 Does Sam's work finish at 6pm?
Yes ☐ No ☐

6 Does he have lunch at 2:30pm?
Yes ☐ No ☐

7 Does he watch TV in the evening?
Yes ☐ No ☐

✉
⌄ ✕

To: Pete

Subject: Life in my new town

Hi Pete,

Let me tell you about life in my new town. I get up at 7am and have a shower. I don't eat breakfast at home, but I eat some fruit at work.

I work in a bank in the town. Work starts at 9:30am and finishes at 6pm, but I have lunch at 1:30pm. In the evening, I eat dinner and watch TV.

Best wishes,
Sam

17.9 COMPLÉTEZ LES PHRASES, PUIS LISEZ-LES À VOIX HAUTE.

___Do___ you go to the movies on Saturdays?

1 _____ you go to a restaurant on Fridays?

2 _____ Peter live near the museum?

3 _____ Sam and Doug work with animals?

4 _____ she get up at 7am on the weekend?

5 _____ they play tennis in the evening?

18 Répondre aux questions

Lorsque vous répondez à une question en anglais, vous pouvez omettre des mots afin d'alléger votre réponse. Ces réponses courtes sont souvent utilisées à l'oral.

⚙ Grammaire Les réponses courtes
Aa Vocabulaire Les métiers et les routines
🧩 Compétence Répondre à des questions à l'oral

18.1 COCHEZ LA RÉPONSE CORRESPONDANT À CHAQUE QUESTION.

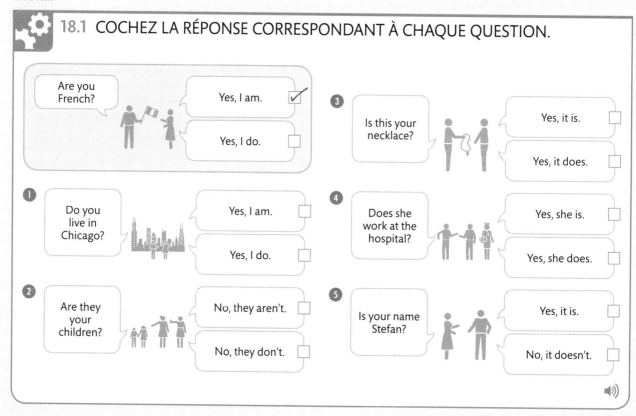

Are you French?
- Yes, I am. ✓
- Yes, I do.

1 Do you live in Chicago?
- Yes, I am.
- Yes, I do.

2 Are they your children?
- No, they aren't.
- No, they don't.

3 Is this your necklace?
- Yes, it is.
- Yes, it does.

4 Does she work at the hospital?
- Yes, she is.
- Yes, she does.

5 Is your name Stefan?
- Yes, it is.
- No, it doesn't.

18.2 COMPLÉTEZ CHAQUE PHRASE AVEC UNE RÉPONSE COURTE APPROPRIÉE.

Is this your cat?
Yes, _____*it is.*_____

1 Do you play golf?
No, _____

2 Is Paula your wife?
Yes, _____

3 Does Peter speak French?
No, _____

4 Do they work at the factory?
No, _____

5 Is Mario from Italy?
Yes, _____

18.3 LISEZ LE COURRIEL, PUIS RÉPONDEZ AUX QUESTIONS.

Does Helen have a new job?

Yes, she does.

1 Is Helen a German teacher?

_____

2 Does Helen start work at 8am?

_____

3 Is Helen's school small?

_____

4 Does Helen finish at 4pm?

_____

5 Does Helen read a book in the evening?

_____

✉   ⌄ ✕

To: Kim

Subject: My new job

Hi Kim,
I have some great news! I have a new job. I'm a French teacher at the school on Palm Avenue. Let me tell you about my typical day.

I get up at 8am and I walk to work. The school is big and has 800 children. I start work at 9am and I have lunch at 1pm. My students are very nice! I finish work at 4pm, and then I walk home. In the evening, I mark up my students' homework, then drink a glass of wine and watch a movie.

Say hello to Bob!
Helen

↩ ⏪   📎 🗑

18.4 ÉCOUTEZ L'ENREGISTREMENT, PUIS COCHEZ LES BONNES RÉPONSES.

Jane commence un nouveau travail d'enseignante. Elle rencontre Bob qui enseigne dans la même école.

Jane is a teacher.
True ☑ **False** ☐ **Not given** ☐

1 Bob is an English teacher.
True ☐ **False** ☐ **Not given** ☐

2 Jane is from Dublin.
True ☐ **False** ☐ **Not given** ☐

3 Jane's husband is a teacher too.
True ☐ **False** ☐ **Not given** ☐

4 Jane's husband works near their house.
True ☐ **False** ☐ **Not given** ☐

5 Jane's husband starts work at 8:30am.
True ☐ **False** ☐ **Not given** ☐

6 Bob plays tennis every weekend.
True ☐ **False** ☐ **Not given** ☐

7 Jane goes to the movies a lot.
True ☐ **False** ☐ **Not given** ☐

19 Poser des questions

Utilisez des mots interrogatifs tels que « what », « who », « when » et « where » pour poser des questions ouvertes auxquelles on ne peut pas répondre par « yes » ou « no ».

⚙ **Grammaire** Les questions ouvertes
Aa Vocabulaire Les mots interrogatifs
🧩 **Compétence** Demander des précisions

Aa 19.1 RELIEZ CHAQUE QUESTION À LA RÉPONSE CORRESPONDANTE.

When is your birthday? → It's on January 24.

It's half past seven.

1 What is your name?

2 How are you? — It's his birthday.

3 What is the time? — It's on Saturday.

4 Who is that woman? — I'm fine, thanks.

5 Where is the café? — He's the boy with red hair.

6 Why is Ben happy? — It's at 3 o'clock.

7 Which one is your brother? — It's across from the bank.

8 What time is your meeting? — Franco. And yours?

9 When is your party? — I'm twenty-three.

10 How old are you? — That's my wife, Vicky.

🔊

⚙ 19.2 COMPLÉTEZ LES QUESTIONS AVEC LES MOTS DE LA LISTE.

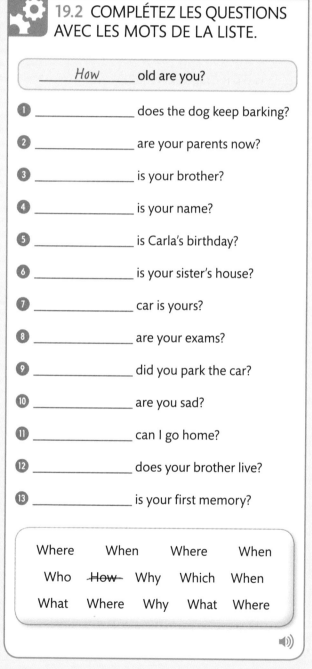

_____How_____ old are you?

1 _____ does the dog keep barking?

2 _____ are your parents now?

3 _____ is your brother?

4 _____ is your name?

5 _____ is Carla's birthday?

6 _____ is your sister's house?

7 _____ car is yours?

8 _____ are your exams?

9 _____ did you park the car?

10 _____ are you sad?

11 _____ can I go home?

12 _____ does your brother live?

13 _____ is your first memory?

Where	When	Where	When
Who	~~How~~	Why	Which	When
What	Where	Why	What	Where

🔊

19.3 ÉCOUTEZ L'ENREGISTREMENT, PUIS COCHEZ LES BONNES RÉPONSES.

Greg parle des membres de sa famille.

What is Greg's grandmother's name?

Shelley ☐
Ellie ☑
Emma ☐

❶ How old is Greg's grandmother?

84 years old ☐
82 years old ☐
83 years old ☐

❷ Where does she live?

Near the church ☐
Near the cathedral ☐
Near the supermarket ☐

❸ Where does Greg's mother work?

At a school ☐
At a museum ☐
At a theater ☐

❹ What does Greg's mother do?

She's a cleaner ☐
She's a receptionist ☐
She's a teacher ☐

❺ How old is Samantha?

21 ☐
19 ☐
23 ☐

19.4 ÉCRIVEZ LES MOTS SUIVANTS DANS LE BON ORDRE AFIN DE RECONSTITUER LES PHRASES.

| wake | do | you | up? | When |

When do you wake up?

❶ | you | shirt | do | Which | prefer? |

_____

❷ | son | does | go | your | to | college? | Where |

_____

❸ | get | How | do | you | to | work? |

_____

❹ | go | you | Where | swimming? | do |

_____

❺ | bed? | you | What | do | time | go | to |

_____

❻ | start | does | When | work? | Jane |

_____

❼ | for | do | What | you | eat | breakfast? |

_____

19.5 COMPLÉTEZ LES QUESTIONS AVEC LES MOTS DE LA LISTE, PUIS LISEZ-LES À VOIX HAUTE.

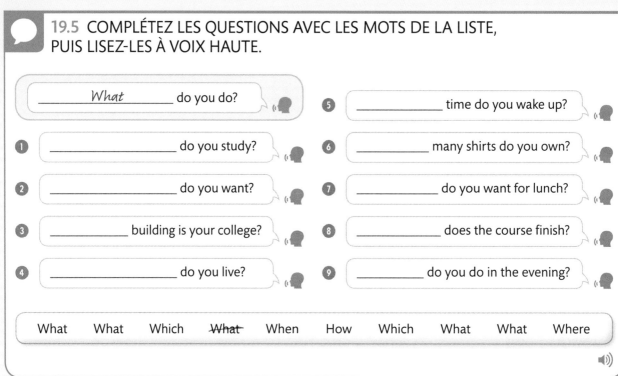

_____*What*_____ do you do?

1 _____ do you study?

2 _____ do you want?

3 _____ building is your college?

4 _____ do you live?

5 _____ time do you wake up?

6 _____ many shirts do you own?

7 _____ do you want for lunch?

8 _____ does the course finish?

9 _____ do you do in the evening?

What   What   Which   ~~What~~   When   How   Which   What   What   Where

19.6 RÉCRIVEZ LES PHRASES EN CORRIGEANT LES ERREURS.

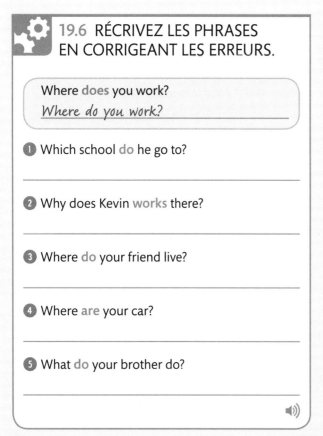

Where **does** you work?
Where do you work?

1 Which school **do** he go to?

_____

2 Why does Kevin **works** there?

_____

3 Where **do** your friend live?

_____

4 Where **are** your car?

_____

5 What **do** your brother do?

_____

19.7 RÉCRIVEZ LES PHRASES À LA FORME INTERROGATIVE.

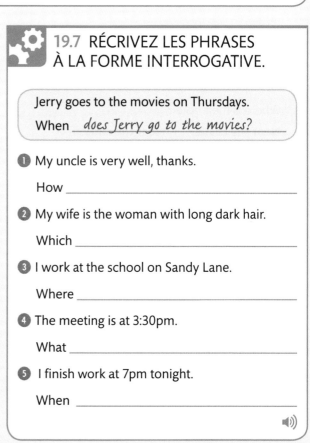

Jerry goes to the movies on Thursdays.
When _does Jerry go to the movies?_

1 My uncle is very well, thanks.

How _____

2 My wife is the woman with long dark hair.

Which _____

3 I work at the school on Sandy Lane.

Where _____

4 The meeting is at 3:30pm.

What _____

5 I finish work at 7pm tonight.

When _____

19.8 UTILISEZ LE SCHÉMA POUR CRÉER 12 PHRASES, PUIS LISEZ-LES À VOIX HAUTE.

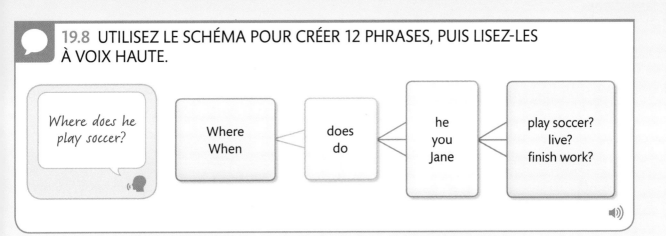

Where does he play soccer?

Where	does	he	play soccer?
When	do	you	live?
		Jane	finish work?

19.9 LISEZ LE COURRIEL, PUIS COCHEZ LES BONNES RÉPONSES.

Which country are Tim and Janet in?
France ✓ **Italy** ☐

1 What is the name of the town?
Blois ☐ **Tours** ☐

2 Who is Tim with?
Janet ☐ **Claire** ☐

3 Where is their hotel?
Near the castle ☐ **Near the cathedral** ☐

4 What do they eat for breakfast?
Cereal ☐ **French bread** ☐

5 Where do they drink their coffee?
In the hotel ☐ **In a café** ☐

6 What do they do in the afternoon?
Explore the old town ☐ **Visit a restaurant** ☐

7 How old is the castle?
About 200 years old ☐ **About 1,000 years old** ☐

8 What can you see at the castle?
Some beautiful paintings ☐ **Historic furniture** ☐

✉ ⌄ ✕

To: Claire

Subject: Having fun!

Hello Claire,

We're on vacation in France this week! We're in Blois, a small town near Tours. I am here with Janet, an old friend from school. Our hotel is near the castle in the old town, and is not far from some nice cafés and restaurants. We eat French bread for breakfast every morning, and I buy it from a local bakery. In the morning, Janet and I go for coffee in a local café and eat a pastry. French pastries are delicious. In the afternoon, we walk by the river and explore the old town. There are some excellent stores, so I'll get you a present. The castle is amazing. It's about 1,000 years old and has lots of rooms with beautiful paintings.

See you soon!
Tim

20 Vocabulaire

Aa 20.1 **EN VILLE** PLACEZ LES MOTS DE LA LISTE SOUS L'IMAGE CORRESPONDANTE.

village

① _____

② _____

③ _____

④ _____

⑦ _____

⑧ _____

⑨ _____

⑩ _____

⑪ _____

⑭ _____

⑮ _____

⑯ _____

⑰ _____

⑱ _____

㉑ _____

㉒ _____

㉓ _____

㉔ _____

㉕ _____

5 _____

6 _____

12 _____

13 _____

19 _____

20 _____

26 _____

27 _____

supermarket   pharmacy

far   hospital   bus station

library   café   post office

here   ~~village~~   town

park   castle   airport

police station   there   bank

bridge   factory   bar

mosque   train station   near

hotel   school   office building

swimming pool   restaurant

🔊

Parler de votre ville

Lorsque vous parlez de la présence de quelque chose, vous pouvez utiliser « there is » pour une chose et « there are » pour plusieurs. Les formes négatives sont « there isn't » et « there aren't ».

⚙ **Grammaire** « There is » et « there are »
Aa Vocabulaire Les villes et les bâtiments
🧩 **Compétence** Décrire une ville

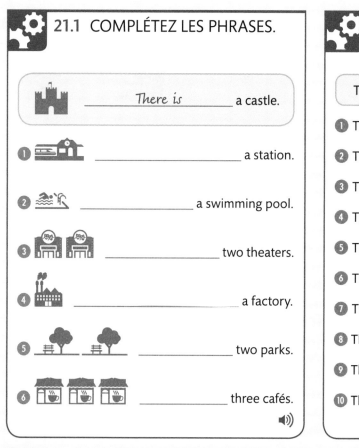

21.1 COMPLÉTEZ LES PHRASES.

_____There is_____ a castle.

1 _____ a station.

2 _____ a swimming pool.

3 _____ two theaters.

4 _____ a factory.

5 _____ two parks.

6 _____ three cafés.

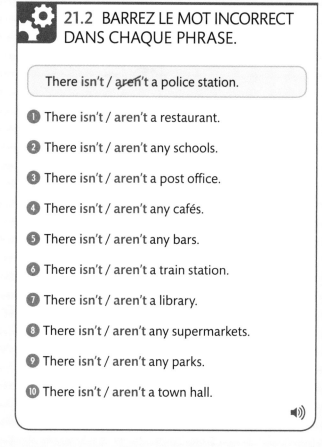

21.2 BARREZ LE MOT INCORRECT DANS CHAQUE PHRASE.

There isn't / aren't a police station.

1 There isn't / aren't a restaurant.

2 There isn't / aren't any schools.

3 There isn't / aren't a post office.

4 There isn't / aren't any cafés.

5 There isn't / aren't any bars.

6 There isn't / aren't a train station.

7 There isn't / aren't a library.

8 There isn't / aren't any supermarkets.

9 There isn't / aren't any parks.

10 There isn't / aren't a town hall.

21.3 UTILISEZ LE SCHÉMA POUR CRÉER 8 PHRASES, PUIS LISEZ-LES À VOIX HAUTE.

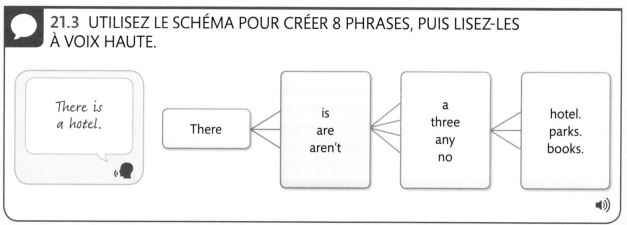

There is a hotel.

| There | is / are / aren't | a / three / any / no | hotel. / parks. / books. |

21.4 ÉCOUTEZ L'ENREGISTREMENT, PUIS NUMÉROTEZ LES IMAGES DANS LE BON ORDRE.

21.5 METTEZ LES PHRASES SUIVANTES À LA FORME NÉGATIVE.

There is a theater.	=	*There isn't a theater.*
❶ There is a school.	=	
❷ There are two churches.	=	
❸ There is a café.	=	
❹ There is a library.	=	
❺ There are two airports.	=	
❻ There are three hotels.	=	
❼ There are two parks.	=	
❽ There is a town hall.	=	

🔊

21.6 ÉCOUTEZ L'ENREGISTREMENT, PUIS COCHEZ LES BONNES RÉPONSES.

Gordon décrit la ville dans laquelle il vit avec sa famille.

Melcome is in...
Scotland. ☐
Canada. ☑
England. ☐
New Zealand. ☐

1 There are two ...... in Melcome.
post offices ☐
banks ☐
churches ☐
offices ☐

2 Gordon works in a...
museum. ☐
café. ☐
factory. ☐
primary school. ☐

3 In the evening Gordon goes to a...
library. ☐
café. ☐
restaurant. ☐
swimming pool. ☐

4 Gordon's wife works in a...
hospital. ☐
theater. ☐
store. ☐
post office. ☐

5 Gordon's son is a...
teacher. ☐
doctor. ☐
police officer. ☐
actor. ☐

21.7 ÉCRIVEZ LES MOTS SUIVANTS DANS LE BON ORDRE AFIN DE RECONSTITUER LES PHRASES.

| are | three | cafés. | There |

There are three cafés.

3 | hotels. | are | There | no |

_____

1 | supermarket. | is | a | There |

_____

4 | There | three | are | schools. |

_____

2 | restaurants. | There | any | aren't |

_____

5 | is | station. | a | There | bus |

_____

🔊

21.8 LISEZ LE COURRIEL, PUIS COCHEZ LES BONNES RÉPONSES.

There are two beaches.
True ☐ **False** ☑

❶ There isn't a castle.
True ☐ **False** ☐

❷ There is a park.
True ☐ **False** ☐

❸ There is a supermarket.
True ☐ **False** ☐

❹ There aren't any stores.
True ☐ **False** ☐

❺ There is a big restaurant.
True ☐ **False** ☐

❻ There are four cafés.
True ☐ **False** ☐

❼ There is an airport.
True ☐ **False** ☐

✉ ⌄ ✕

To: Christine

Subject: Visiting Westport

Hi Christine,

We are on vacation in Westport and it's beautiful! There's lots to do here for all the family. There aren't any beaches, but there's a castle and a big park. The castle is very old and really interesting. And the children go to the park every day. There isn't a supermarket here, but there are lots of small stores in the center. Anne loves them.

In the evening, I walk with Anne and the children in the center. There is a big fish restaurant here. I like fish a lot! There are also three cafés where we relax. It's easy to get to Westport. The airport is not far from the center and there's a bus station near our hotel.

Wish you were here!
See you soon!
Tom

↩ ↩↩ 📎 🗑

21.9 OBSERVEZ L'IMAGE, COMPLÉTEZ LES PHRASES, PUIS LISEZ-LES À VOIX HAUTE.

There is a library.

❶ _____ stores.

❷ _____ castles.

❸ _____ a church.

❹ _____ a hospital.

❺ _____ a post office.

🔊

22 « A » et « the »

Utilisez l'article défini (« the ») ou indéfini (« a », « an »)
pour parler de choses de manière spécifique ou générale.
Utilisez « some » pour parler de plusieurs choses.

⚙ **Grammaire** Les articles définis et indéfinis
Aa **Vocabulaire** Les lieux dans la ville
🧩 **Compétence** Les articles

22.1 BARREZ LES MOTS INCORRECTS DANS CHAQUE PHRASE.

 Alex is a / ~~an~~ / ~~the~~ teacher.

5 A / An / The gym is near Sam's house.

1 A / An / The new doctor is called Hilary.

6 There is a / an / the new café in town.

2 Sammy is a / an / the nurse.

7 A / An / The hotel on Elm Lane is nice.

3 There is a / an / the bank downtown.

8 A / An / The new teacher is good.

4 Is there a / an / the hospital near here?

9 There's a / an / the old theater in town.

🔊

22.2 RÉCRIVEZ LES PHRASES SUIVANTES EN CORRIGEANT LES ERREURS.

A new teacher is called Mr. Smith.
The new teacher is called Mr. Smith.

1 I have the sister and the brother.

_____

2 There is the library on Queens Road.

_____

3 I bought a apple and a orange.

_____

4 Is there the bank near here?

_____

5 There is an café at the bus station.

_____

6 My dad is a engineer.

_____

7 There is the cell phone on the table.

_____

🔊

22.3 COMPLÉTEZ LES PHRASES AVEC « A », « AN », « SOME » OU « THE ».

Dear Bob and Sally,

We are in Glenmuir, _____ quiet town in Scotland. There's _____ castle and _____ cathedral here. They're beautiful and _____ castle is really old. There are _____ interesting stores, which we visit every day. We also have _____ new friend here. He's called Alfonso and he works as _____ waiter in _____ Italian restaurant next to _____ shopping mall. He's great!

Jane

22.4 BARREZ LES MOTS INCORRECTS DANS CHAQUE PHRASE.

Is there a / an / any museum in Littleton?

1 Are there a / an / any factories in your town?

2 Is there a / an / any gym downtown?

3 Are there a / an / any pencils in your bag?

4 Is there a / an / any old church on Station Road?

5 Is there a / an / any hospital in the town?

6 Is there a / an / any salon near here?

7 Is there a / an / any apple in the basket?

8 Are there a / an / any restaurants in your town?

9 Is there a / an / any library downtown?

10 Are there a / an / any books on the table?

11 Is there a / an / any café nearby?

12 Is there a / an / any cathedral in that town?

13 Is there a / an / any bank near the supermarket?

14 Are there a / an / any kittens here?

15 Is there a / an / any school in this neighborhood?

◀))

22.5 ÉCRIVEZ LES MOTS SUIVANTS DANS LE BON ORDRE AFIN DE RECONSTITUER LES PHRASES.

some | in | town. | are | my | There | banks

There are some banks in my town.

1. Is | here? | supermarket | there | near | a

_____

2. There | cafés | Beech Road. | some | are | on

_____

3. horses | on | farm. | There | Frank's | are | some

_____

4. airport. | near | There | some | the | are | hotels

_____

22.6 COMPLÉTEZ LES PHRASES, PUIS LISEZ-LES À VOIX HAUTE.

Are ____there any____ stores?

1. Is _____ museum?

2. Are _____ cafés?

3. Are _____ parks near here?

4. Is _____ mosque in the town?

5. Is _____ airport in Saltforth?

6. Are _____ factories in Halford?

7. Is _____ castle in your town?

22.7 RÉPONDEZ AUX QUESTIONS, PUIS LISEZ-LES À VOIX HAUTE.

Are there any cinemas in Littleton?

No, _____ *there aren't.* _____

④ Is there a park in your town?

No, _____

① Are there any supermarkets in the town?

Yes, _____

⑤ Is there a good restaurant near the park?

Yes, _____

② Is there a church on Duke Road?

No, _____

⑥ Are there any castles near your town?

No, _____

③ Are there any theaters near the hotel?

Yes, _____

⑦ Are there any bars and cafés downtown?

Yes, _____

22.8 ÉCOUTEZ L'ENREGISTREMENT, PUIS COCHEZ LES BONNES RÉPONSES.

James décrit sa vie à la ferme.

Where does James live?
on a farm ☑ in a city ☐ in a town ☐

④ What restaurant does Stonehill have?
Italian ☐ French ☐ Mexican ☐

① Where is the museum?
Stonehill ☐ Eastford ☐ There isn't one ☐

⑤ Are there any theaters in Stonehill?
some ☐ none ☐ lots ☐

② Where does James go on the weekend?
theater ☐ church ☐ museum ☐

⑥ How many churches are there in Eastford?
two ☐ four ☐ six ☐

③ Are there any stores in Stonehill?
some ☐ none ☐ lots ☐

⑦ Are there any stores in Eastford?
some ☐ none ☐ lots ☐

Utilisez l'impératif pour ordonner à quelqu'un de faire quelque chose. L'impératif permet également d'avertir une personne d'un danger ou de lui indiquer une direction.

⚙ **Grammaire** L'impératif
Aa Vocabulaire Les directions
🧩 **Compétence** Trouver votre chemin

23.1 RÉCRIVEZ LES VERBES SUIVANTS À L'IMPÉRATIF.

he takes = *take*

1 to put =

2 I read =

3 she works =

4 to start =

5 you eat =

6 they have =

7 it stops =

8 to wake up =

9 we run =

10 they come =

11 you are =

🔊

23.2 IMPÉRATIF OU PRÉSENT SIMPLE ? COCHEZ LA BONNE RÉPONSE.

Eat your breakfast.
imperative ☑ **present simple** ☐

1 I eat my dinner at 6pm.
imperative ☐ **present simple** ☐

2 Come with me.
imperative ☐ **present simple** ☐

3 You read your book every day.
imperative ☐ **present simple** ☐

4 Give that to me.
imperative ☐ **present simple** ☐

5 Read this book.
imperative ☐ **present simple** ☐

6 Eat your dinner.
imperative ☐ **present simple** ☐

7 She goes to bed at 9pm.
imperative ☐ **present simple** ☐

8 I start school at 9am.
imperative ☐ **present simple** ☐

9 Go to bed.
imperative ☐ **present simple** ☐

🔊

23.3 COCHEZ LES DIRECTIONS QUI VOUS MÈNENT À L'ENDROIT INDIQUÉ SUR LA CARTE.

You are here

For the hospital...
Take the first left. The hospital is on the left ☑
Take the first left. The hospital is on the right. ☐

1 For the swimming pool...
Go straight ahead. The swimming pool is opposite the castle. ☐
Go straight ahead. The swimming pool is opposite the station. ☐

2 For the school...
Take the second left. The school is opposite the factory. ☐
Take the third left. The school is next to the factory. ☐

3 For the church...
Turn right and take the second right. The church is opposite the hotel. ☐
Turn right and take the first left. The church is opposite the hotel. ☐

4 For the theater...
Take the third left and go straight ahead. The theater is on the right. ☐
Take the third right and go straight ahead. The theater is on the left. ☐

🔊

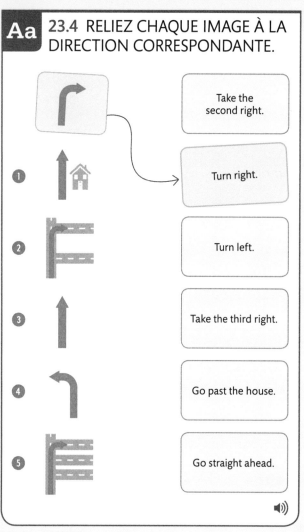

Aa 23.4 RELIEZ CHAQUE IMAGE À LA DIRECTION CORRESPONDANTE.

Take the second right.

Turn right.

Turn left.

Take the third right.

Go past the house.

Go straight ahead.

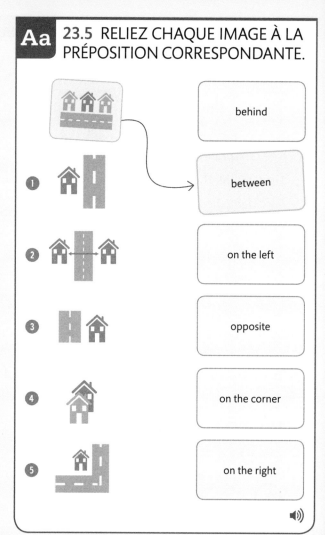

Aa 23.5 RELIEZ CHAQUE IMAGE À LA PRÉPOSITION CORRESPONDANTE.

behind

between

on the left

opposite

on the corner

on the right

23.6 TRANSFORMEZ CES AFFIRMATIONS EN NÉGATIONS.

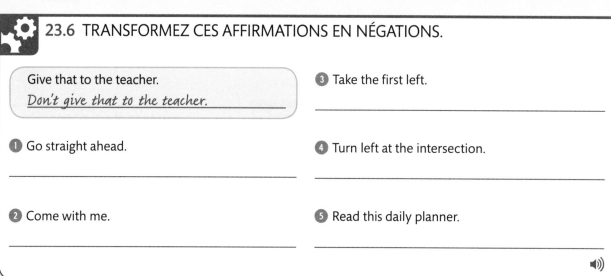

Give that to the teacher.
Don't give that to the teacher.

❶ Go straight ahead.

_____

❷ Come with me.

_____

❸ Take the first left.

_____

❹ Turn left at the intersection.

_____

❺ Read this daily planner.

_____

23.7 ÉCOUTEZ L'ENREGISTREMENT, PUIS NUMÉROTEZ LES DIRECTIONS DANS LE BON ORDRE.

Turn left and the theater is on your right across from the church. ☐ 1

A The café is on the corner next to the church. ☐

B The restaurant is on the right next to the bank. ☐

C Go straight ahead and take the second road on your right. ☐

D Turn right, then take the first left. ☐

E Go past the hotel and the café is on the left. ☐

F The hospital is on the corner on the left. ☐

G Go straight ahead and it's the fourth road on the right. ☐

H Go straight ahead and take the third left. ☐

23.8 OBSERVEZ LES IMAGES, PUIS RÉPONDEZ AUX QUESTIONS EN UTILISANT LA PRÉPOSITION DE LA LISTE CORRESPONDANTE.

The supermarket is
____next to____ the hotel.

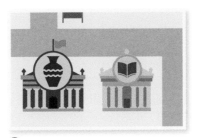

1 The museum is
_____ the library.

2 The restaurant is
_____ the store.

3 The hospital is
_____ the theater.

4 The post office is
_____ the school.

in front of   behind

~~next to~~

opposite   next to

77

24 Relier les phrases

« And » et « but » sont des conjonctions : des mots qui relient des phrases. « And » permet d'ajouter des éléments à une phrase ou de relier des phrases. « But » introduit un contraste.

⚙ **Grammaire** « And » et « but »
Aa Vocabulaire La ville, les métiers et la famille
🧩 **Compétence** Relier les phrases

Aa 24.1 RELIEZ CHAQUE DÉBUT DE PHRASE À LA FIN CORRESPONDANTE.

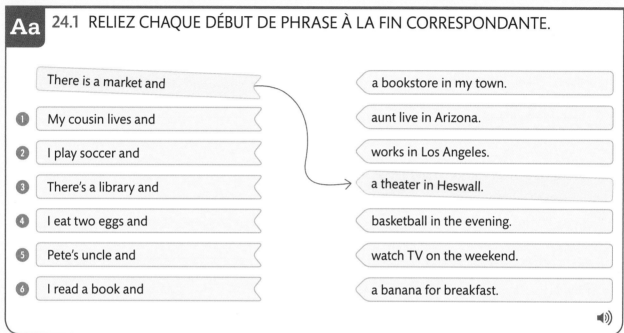

There is a market and → a theater in Heswall.

1. My cousin lives and
2. I play soccer and
3. There's a library and
4. I eat two eggs and
5. Pete's uncle and
6. I read a book and

a bookstore in my town.
aunt live in Arizona.
works in Los Angeles.
a theater in Heswall.
basketball in the evening.
watch TV on the weekend.
a banana for breakfast.

24.2 ÉCOUTEZ L'ENREGISTREMENT, PUIS RELIEZ LES 2 LIEUX QUE LE LOCUTEUR DÉCRIT.

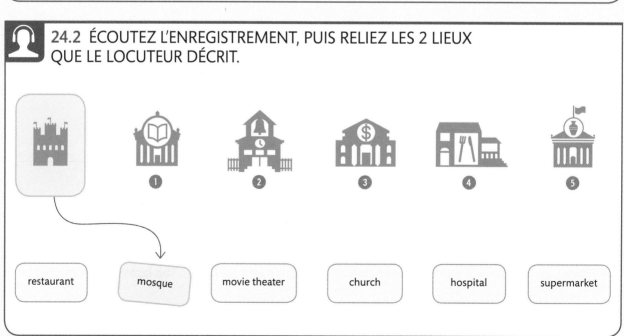

1 2 3 4 5

restaurant | mosque | movie theater | church | hospital | supermarket

24.3 COCHEZ LES PHRASES CORRECTES.

There's a library, a store, and a museum. ☑
There's a library, and a store, a museum. ☐

① Three chefs, four waiters work in my hotel. ☐
Three chefs and four waiters work in my hotel. ☐

② There's a park, a café, and a theater in Pella. ☐
There's a park, a café, a theater in Pella. ☐

③ I have one aunt, and two sisters, and a niece. ☐
I have one aunt, two sisters, and a niece. ☐

④ Ben eats breakfast, and lunch and dinner. ☐
Ben eats breakfast, lunch, and dinner. ☐

⑤ I play and tennis and soccer. ☐
I play tennis and soccer. ☐

⑥ We have and dog and a cat. ☐
We have a dog and a cat. ☐

⑦ I read a book, take a bath on Sundays. ☐
I read a book and take a bath on Sundays. ☐

⑧ Jen speaks French, Spanish, Japanese. ☐
Jen speaks French, Spanish, and Japanese. ☐

⑨ Pete has two dogs and a cat. ☐
Pete has two dogs, a cat. ☐

🔊

24.4 RÉCRIVEZ LES PHRASES SUIVANTES EN LES RELIANT AVEC « AND » OU « BUT ».

I get up. I take a shower.
I get up and take a shower.

① This is my brother. These are my sisters.
_____

② I speak English. I don't speak French.
_____

③ I play video games. I watch TV.
_____

④ I have one uncle. I don't have any aunts.
_____

⑤ There are two stores. There are three hotels.
_____

⑥ I eat lunch every day. I don't eat breakfast.
_____

⑦ There's a hotel. There isn't a store.
_____

⑧ I have a sandwich. I have an apple.
_____

⑨ This is my house. These aren't my keys.
_____

⑩ Those are Sarah's magazines. That is her ID card.
_____

⑪ This phone is Joe's. This laptop isn't Joe's.
_____

🔊

24.5 BARREZ LA CONJONCTION INCORRECTE DANS CHAQUE PHRASE.

I work every weekday ~~and~~/ but not on weekends.

1 There's a library, a store, and / but a café.

2 There's a castle and a church and / but there isn't a museum.

3 Pete eats apples and / but doesn't eat bananas.

4 Greg reads magazines and / but a newspaper.

5 I have a calendar and / but a notebook.

6 He goes swimming and / but he doesn't play soccer.

24.6 COMPLÉTEZ LES PHRASES, PUIS LISEZ-LES À VOIX HAUTE.

My mom _____*and*_____ dad work as doctors in the hospital.

1 Meg likes this restaurant _____ she doesn't like that café.

2 There are two schools _____ there isn't a library in my town.

3 I have a pen, a notebook, _____ a calendar in my bag.

4 My sister goes to the gym on Mondays _____ Thursdays.

5 Pedro works in a school _____ he isn't a teacher.

25 Décrire des lieux

Utilisez des adjectifs pour donner des informations supplémentaires sur un nom ; pour décrire une personne, un bâtiment ou un lieu, par exemple.

⚙ **Grammaire** Les adjectifs
Aa Vocabulaire Les adjectifs et les noms de lieux
🧩 **Compétence** Décrire des lieux

25.1 ÉCRIVEZ LES MOTS SUIVANTS DANS LE BON ORDRE AFIN DE RECONSTITUER LES PHRASES.

castle. | is | old | This | an

This is an old castle.

③ friend | beautiful | a | woman. | My | is

_____

① a | man. | I | busy | am

_____

④ old | cat. | We | a | have | very

_____

② is | a | There | restaurant. | new

_____

⑤ clothes. | are | new | my | These

_____

🔊

25.2 TROUVEZ 8 ADJECTIFS DANS LE COURRIEL ET ÉCRIVEZ-LES.

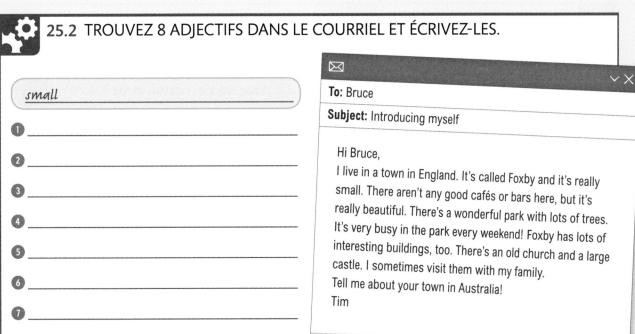

small

① _____

② _____

③ _____

④ _____

⑤ _____

⑥ _____

⑦ _____

✉

∨ ✕

To: Bruce

Subject: Introducing myself

Hi Bruce,

I live in a town in England. It's called Foxby and it's really small. There aren't any good cafés or bars here, but it's really beautiful. There's a wonderful park with lots of trees. It's very busy in the park every weekend! Foxby has lots of interesting buildings, too. There's an old church and a large castle. I sometimes visit them with my family.
Tell me about your town in Australia!
Tim

↩ ↩↩   📎 🗑

25.3 RÉCRIVEZ LA PHRASE DE 2 MANIÈRES DIFFÉRENTES.

Paris is a beautiful city. _The city is beautiful._ _It is beautiful._

① They are small children. _____ _____

② Peter is a good waiter. _____ _____

③ Fido is a big dog. _____ _____

④ Melby is a quiet town. _____ _____

Aa 25.4 RELIEZ CHAQUE ADJECTIF À SON CONTRAIRE.

busy → easy

① old → quiet

② small — bad

③ good — old

④ horrible — slow

⑤ young — large

⑥ fast — beautiful

⑦ difficult — new

25.5 ÉCOUTEZ L'ENREGISTREMENT, PUIS RÉPONDEZ AUX QUESTIONS.

Braemore is a large town in Scotland.
True ☐ **False** ☐ **Not given** ☑

① There are lots of lakes near Braemore.
True ☐ **False** ☐ **Not given** ☐

② There are a few old buildings.
True ☐ **False** ☐ **Not given** ☐

③ Braemore has only a few hotels.
True ☐ **False** ☐ **Not given** ☐

④ Kirsty works in a large hotel.
True ☐ **False** ☐ **Not given** ☐

⑤ Kirsty is not very busy on weekends.
True ☐ **False** ☐ **Not given** ☐

⑥ Kirsty goes to a café with her friends.
True ☐ **False** ☐ **Not given** ☐

25.6 COMPLÉTEZ LES PHRASES, PUIS LISEZ-LES À VOIX HAUTE.

The lakes _are_ beautiful _and the_ beaches _are_ quiet.

1. _____ sea _____ blue _____ sun _____ hot.

2. _____ beach _____ busy _____ hotels _____ ugly.

3. _____ city _____ old _____ buildings _____ beautiful.

4. _____ restaurant _____ good _____ waiter _____ friendly.

5. _____ countryside _____ beautiful _____ mountains _____ large.

6. _____ town _____ small _____ shops _____ quiet.

Aa 25.7 COMPLÉTEZ LES PHRASES AVEC LES MOTS DE LA LISTE.

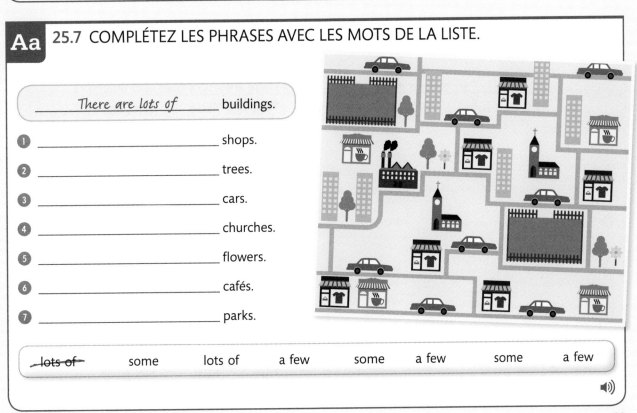

There are lots of buildings.

1. _____ shops.

2. _____ trees.

3. _____ cars.

4. _____ churches.

5. _____ flowers.

6. _____ cafés.

7. _____ parks.

~~lots of~~   some   lots of   a few   some   a few   some   a few

26 Donner des raisons

Utilisez la conjonction « because » pour donner une raison. Vous pouvez aussi utiliser « because » pour répondre à la question « Why? ».

⚙ **Grammaire** « Because »
Aa **Vocabulaire** Les lieux et les métiers
🧩 **Compétence** Donner des raisons

Aa 26.1 RELIEZ CHAQUE DÉBUT DE PHRASE À LA FIN CORRESPONDANTE.

I work at night because

1. Fred works outside because
2. Mick travels to Switzerland because
3. Saul goes to bed late because
4. I get up at 5am because
5. Marion goes to the library because
6. Colin works with children because

he's a teacher.

she's a student.

I'm a mailman.

I'm a night nurse.

he goes skiing there.

he works in a restaurant.

he's a farmer.

🔊

🎧 26.2 ÉCOUTEZ L'ENREGISTREMENT, PUIS COCHEZ LA BONNE RÉPONSE.

Leo uses a computer because...
he works in an office ☑ **he works on a farm** ☐

1. Rick works outside because...
he's a gardener ☐ **he's a farmer** ☐

2. Mary Lou works with children because...
she's a teacher ☐ **she's a nurse** ☐

3. Carl goes to the library because...
he's a student ☐ **he's a professor** ☐

4. Sally gets up at 6am because...
she goes running ☐ **she goes to the gym** ☐

5. Pete works at the theater because...
he's an actor ☐ **he's a receptionist** ☐

6. Michael has not come to work because...
he's out of town ☐ **he has the flu** ☐

7. Sana works in a restaurant because...
she's a chef ☐ **she's a waitress** ☐

26.3 COMPLÉTEZ LES PHRASES AVEC LES MOTS DE LA LISTE.

John goes to the restaurant because _____ *it has delicious food* _____.

1. Aziz lives in the countryside because _____.

2. We don't have breakfast because _____.

3. Mr. Aspinall gets up early because _____.

4. Arnold wears a suit because _____.

5. Vicky works outside because _____.

6. I work in a hospital because _____.

he thinks it's beautiful	~~it has delicious food~~	we're very busy	I'm a doctor
he takes his dog for a walk	he works in a bank	she is a gardener	

🔊

26.4 UTILISEZ LE SCHÉMA POUR CRÉER 6 PHRASES, PUIS LISEZ-LES À VOIX HAUTE.

Clara works in a theater because she is an actor.

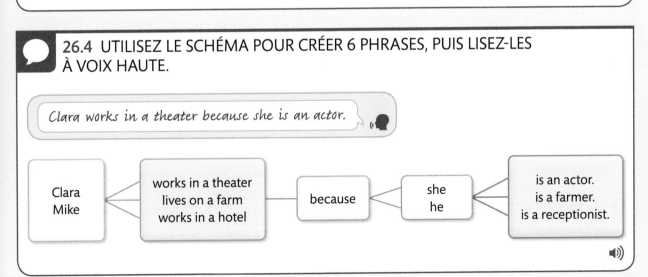

| Clara Mike | works in a theater / lives on a farm / works in a hotel | because | she / he | is an actor. / is a farmer. / is a receptionist. |

🔊

Aa 27.1 **DANS LA MAISON** PLACEZ LES MOTS DE LA LISTE SOUS L'IMAGE CORRESPONDANTE.

desk

 ❶ _____

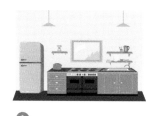 ❷ _____

 ❸ _____

 ❽ _____

 ❾ _____

 ❿ _____

 ⓫ _____

 ⓰ _____

 ⓱ _____

 ⓲ _____

 ⓳ _____

couch (US) / sofa (UK)   dining room   toilet   house   closet (US) / wardrobe (UK)

bathroom   bedroom   ~~desk~~   chair   bathtub   table   bookcase

4 _____

5 _____

6 _____

7 _____

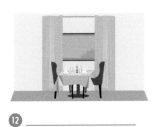

12 _____

13 _____

14 _____

15 _____

20 _____

21 _____

22 _____

23 _____

kitchen   door   armchair   study   garage   apartment block (US) / block of flats (UK)

lamp   television   bed   shower   window   refrigerator (US) / fridge (UK)

28 Ce que vous possédez

Vous pouvez utiliser le verbe « to have » lorsque vous parlez de choses que vous possédez, telles que des meubles ou des animaux domestiques. Vous pouvez également employer ce verbe pour parler de vos diplômes, d'appareils électroménagers ou des pièces de votre maison.

 Grammaire « Have »

Aa Vocabulaire Les objets dans la maiso

Compétence Parler de ce que vous possèdez

28.1 BARREZ LE MOT INCORRECT DANS CHAQUE PHRASE.

We **have** / ~~has~~ a car in the garage.

 ① My friend **have** / **has** new glasses.

 ② John **have** / **has** two dogs.

 ③ We **have** / **has** an old castle in our city.

 ④ They **have** / **has** a lot of parks in their town.

 ⑤ I **have** / **has** a beautiful necklace.

 ⑥ Alex **have** / **has** a new camera.

 ⑦ Our house **have** / **has** a lovely yard.

 ⑧ Phil and Sue **have** / **has** four daughters.

 ⑨ Pete **have** / **has** a new cell phone.

 ⑩ Your town **have** / **has** a big hotel.

 ⑪ I **have** / **has** a lot of friends.

28.2 COMPLÉTEZ LES PHRASES AVEC « HAS » OU « HAVE ».

They ____*have*____ two daughters.

① Bob and Shirley _____ a big dog.

② She _____ some new friends.

③ We _____ two sons at home.

④ James _____ two cars.

⑤ His house _____ three bedrooms.

⑥ Pam _____ lots of books at home.

⑦ He _____ two cats.

⑧ Sally's house _____ a new kitchen.

⑨ You _____ a beautiful house.

⑩ I _____ three sisters.

⑪ Kelly and Mark _____ a microwave.

⑫ We _____ a castle in our town.

⑬ Sanjay _____ a cat and a dog.

⑭ You _____ three brothers.

⑮ Ross _____ a new cell phone.

⑯ Our house _____ two bathrooms.

⑰ I _____ a couch in my room.

⑱ Washington _____ some lovely parks.

28.3 COCHEZ LES PHRASES CORRECTES.

We have apples and oranges. ☑
We apples and oranges have. ☐

1 I have two sisters. ☐
I has two sisters. ☐

2 You has a beautiful house. ☐
You have a beautiful house. ☐

3 We a garden have. ☐
We have a garden. ☐

4 Sam and Greg have a dog. ☐
Sam and Greg has a dog. ☐

5 Marlon a brother has. ☐
Marlon has a brother. ☐

6 Fardale have an old castle. ☐
Fardale has an old castle. ☐

7 They have a new car. ☐
They has a new car. ☐

28.4 LISEZ LES ANNONCES, PUIS COCHEZ LA BONNE RÉPONSE.

Ocean View has two bedrooms.
True ☐ **False** ☑

1 Ocean View has a garage.
True ☐ **False** ☐

2 Sunny Bank has two bathrooms.
True ☐ **False** ☐

3 There isn't a garage at Sunny Bank.
True ☐ **False** ☐

4 Belle Vue Manor has six bedrooms.
True ☐ **False** ☐

5 Belle Vue Manor has a small yard.
True ☐ **False** ☐

6 Mossfield Cottage has an old kitchen.
True ☐ **False** ☐

7 Mossfield Cottage has a small yard.
True ☐ **False** ☐

PROPERTY

Ocean View $2,000/month
This beautiful house is right on the ocean. There are three bedrooms and a big kitchen. It also has a lovely yard, but there is no garage.

Sunny Bank $1,500/month
This modern apartment has two bedrooms and one bathroom with a bath and a shower. All the furniture is new. There isn't a yard, but there is a garage.

Belle Vue Manor
This large house is in the center of Sunset Cove. It has six bedrooms, three bathrooms, and two garages. There is a big yard with lots of trees and a lake.

Mossfield Cottage $1300/month
This small house is in the old part of Summerwood. It has two bedrooms, a bathroom, and a new kitchen. There is a small yard with lots of beautiful flowers.

28.5 RÉCRIVEZ LES PHRASES SUIVANTES EN UTILISANT LA FORME CONTRACTÉE.

> Sam **does not** have a car.
> _Sam doesn't have a car._

❸ Rob's house **does not** have a garage.

_____

❶ We **do not** have a computer at home.

_____

❹ You **do not** have any sisters.

_____

❷ My city **does not** have a castle.

_____

❺ The village **does not** have any stores.

_____

🔊

 28.6 RÉCRIVEZ CHAQUE PHRASE SANS FORME CONTRACTÉE.

> I **haven't** got a dog.
> _I have not got a dog._

❶ You**'ve** got a beautiful necklace.

_____

❷ She **hasn't** got any sisters.

_____

❸ We **haven't** got a microwave.

_____

❹ Greg **hasn't** got a bike.

_____

❺ My town**'s** got two theaters.

_____

❻ Chloe **hasn't** got a cat.

_____

❼ They**'ve** got a new house.

_____

🔊

28.7 ÉCOUTEZ L'ENREGISTREMENT, PUIS RELIEZ CHAQUE ÉLÉMENT À SON PROPRIÉTAIRE.

Our town

❶ John's sister

❷ Our house

❸ My friend Sam

❹ Adam and I

❺ Sally and Jonathan

28.8 UTILISEZ LE SCHÉMA POUR CRÉER 11 PHRASES, PUIS LISEZ-LES À VOIX HAUTE.

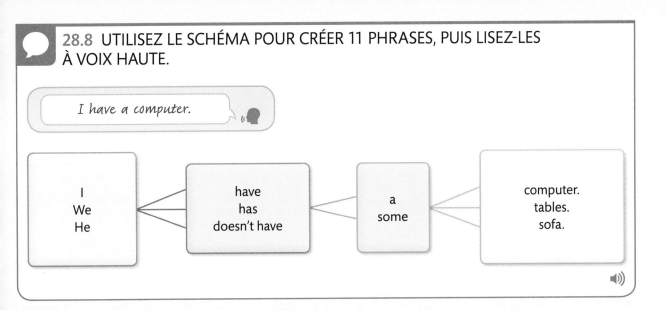

I have a computer.

| I / We / He | have / has / doesn't have | a / some | computer. / tables. / sofa. |

28.9 RÉCRIVEZ LA PHRASE DE 2 MANIÈRES DIFFÉRENTES.

I **have** a car.	I **have got** a car.	I've **got** a car.
①	She **has got** two bedrooms.	
② They **don't have** a dog.		
③		We've **got** some chairs.
④	He **has got** a brother.	
⑤ Carla **doesn't have** a sister.		
⑥	You **have got** a car.	
⑦		Phil's **got** a dog.
⑧ You **have** a yard.		
⑨		Jamal **hasn't got** a sofa.
⑩	They **have got** a shower.	
⑪		May's **got** a couch.
⑫ He **doesn't have** a cat.		

29 Qu'est-ce que vous avez ?

Posez des questions avec « have » pour demander à quelqu'un ce qu'il possède. On utilise « do » ou « does » pour formuler la question.

⚙ **Grammaire** Les questions avec « have »

Aa Vocabulaire La maison et le mobilier

🧩 **Compétence** Poser des questions concernant les objets de la maison

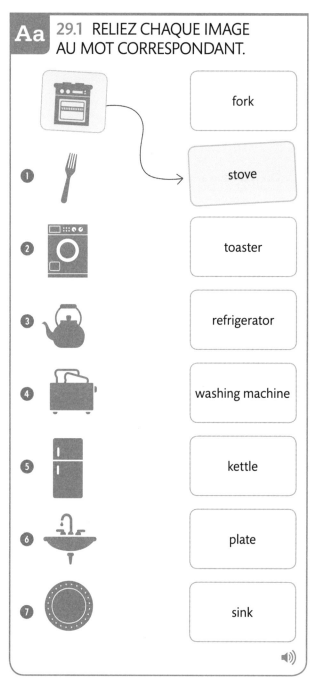

Aa 29.1 RELIEZ CHAQUE IMAGE AU MOT CORRESPONDANT.

fork

stove

toaster

refrigerator

washing machine

kettle

plate

sink

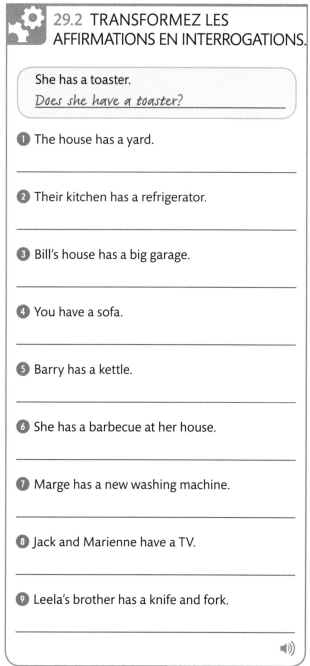

⚙ 29.2 TRANSFORMEZ LES AFFIRMATIONS EN INTERROGATIONS.

She has a toaster.
Does she have a toaster?

❶ The house has a yard.

❷ Their kitchen has a refrigerator.

❸ Bill's house has a big garage.

❹ You have a sofa.

❺ Barry has a kettle.

❻ She has a barbecue at her house.

❼ Marge has a new washing machine.

❽ Jack and Marienne have a TV.

❾ Leela's brother has a knife and fork.

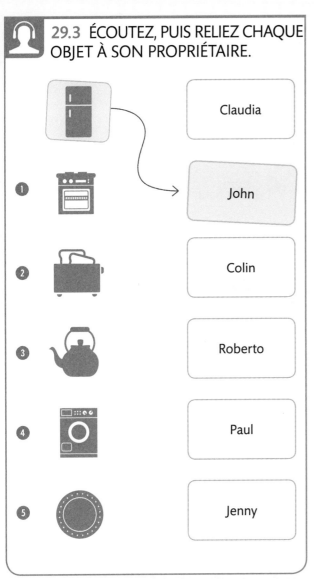

29.3 ÉCOUTEZ, PUIS RELIEZ CHAQUE OBJET À SON PROPRIÉTAIRE.

Claudia

John

Colin

Roberto

Paul

Jenny

❶ ❷ ❸ ❹ ❺

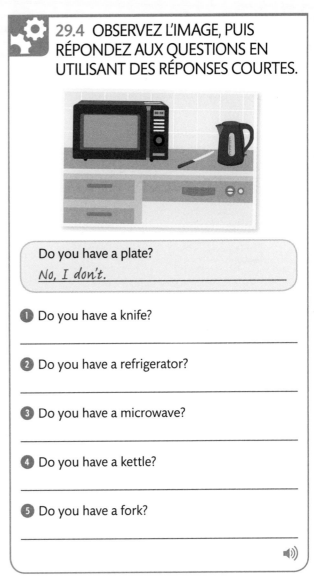

29.4 OBSERVEZ L'IMAGE, PUIS RÉPONDEZ AUX QUESTIONS EN UTILISANT DES RÉPONSES COURTES.

Do you have a plate?
No, I don't.

❶ Do you have a knife?
_____

❷ Do you have a refrigerator?
_____

❸ Do you have a microwave?
_____

❹ Do you have a kettle?
_____

❺ Do you have a fork?
_____

29.5 UTILISEZ LE SCHÉMA POUR CRÉER 9 PHRASES, PUIS LISEZ-LES À VOIX HAUTE.

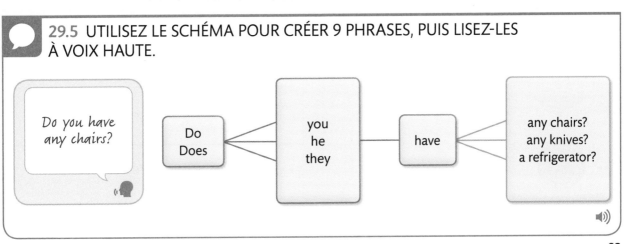

Do you have any chairs?

Do	you	have	any chairs?
Does	he		any knives?
	they		a refrigerator?

29.6 RÉPONDEZ AUX QUESTIONS, PUIS LISEZ LES RÉPONSES À VOIX HAUTE.

Does Kate have a necklace?

No, _____she doesn't_____ .

1 Does Paula have a sofa?

Yes, _____ .

2 Does James have a snake?

Yes, _____ .

3 Does Keith have an umbrella?

No, _____ .

4 Does your town have a library?

Yes, _____ .

5 Do your parents have a car?

No, _____ .

6 Does your mom have a microwave?

No, _____ .

7 Does Gerald have a bottle?

Yes, _____ .

29.7 ÉCRIVEZ LA QUESTION CORRESPONDANT À CHAQUE AFFIRMATION.

She has got a car.
Has she got a car?

1 They have got a microwave.
_____

2 Shaun and Shania have got a pet snake.
_____

3 Charles has got a camera.
_____

4 Clarissa has got a new laptop.
_____

5 Carol's house has got a big yard.
_____

6 Your friends have got my book.
_____

7 Brian has got a new TV.
_____

29.8 RÉCRIVEZ LES QUESTIONS AVEC « HAVE GOT ».

Do you have a dog?
Have you got a dog?

1 Does the kitchen have a microwave?

2 Does your house have a yard?

3 Do the Hendersons have a car?

4 Does Claire have my glasses?

5 Do your parents have a computer?

6 Does Paul have my book?

7 Does Brian have a magazine?

8 Do your neighbors have a basement?

9 Does your cell phone have a camera?

10 Does Sam have any money?

11 Does your town have a supermarket?

12 Does Brian have a sister?

13 Do your children have a cat?

14 Does your husband have a camera?

15 Does your school have a library?

16 Does Jane have a cell phone?

17 Do the kids have their bikes?

◀))

 29.9 UTILISEZ LE SCHÉMA POUR CRÉER 7 PHRASES, PUIS LISEZ-LES À VOIX HAUTE.

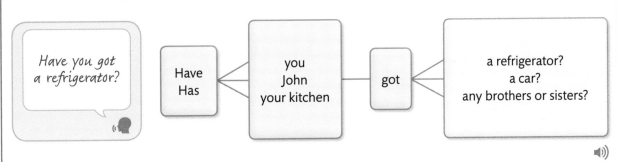

◀))

Aa 30.1 **BOIRE ET MANGER** PLACEZ LES MOTS DE LA LISTE SOUS L'IMAGE CORRESPONDANTE.

food

① _____

② _____

③ _____

④ _____

⑧ _____

⑨ _____

⑩ _____

⑪ _____

⑫ _____

⑯ _____

⑰ _____

⑱ _____

⑲ _____

⑳ _____

㉔ _____

㉕ _____

㉖ _____

㉗ _____

㉘ _____

5 _____

6 _____

7 _____

13 _____

14 _____

15 _____

21 _____

22 _____

23 _____

29 _____

30 _____

31 _____

meat   breakfast

sugar   potatoes

bread   fruit   cheese

vegetables   drinks

strawberry   juice

apple   seafood

butter   chocolate

spaghetti   orange

water   coffee

pasta   milk

lunch   burger

eggs   ~~food~~

rice   fish   dinner

salad   cereal

banana   cake

31 Compter

En anglais, les noms peuvent être soit dénombrables, soit indénombrables. Les noms dénombrables peuvent être comptés individuellement. Les noms qui ne peuvent pas être séparés et comptés sont indénombrables.

Grammaire Les noms indénombrables
Aa Vocabulaire Les récipients alimentaires
Compétence Parler de nourriture

31.1 ÉCRIVEZ LES MOTS DE LA LISTE DANS L'ENCADRÉ CORRESPONDANT.

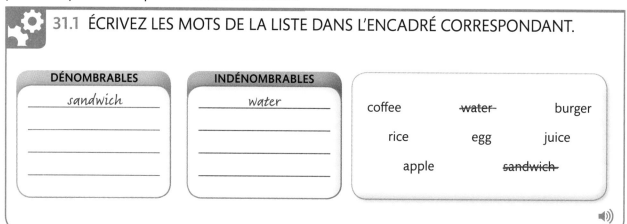

DÉNOMBRABLES

sandwich

INDÉNOMBRABLES

water

coffee	~~water~~	burger
rice	egg	juice
apple	~~sandwich~~	

31.2 BARREZ LE MOT INCORRECT DANS CHAQUE PHRASE.

Bob has ~~a~~ / **some** sugar.

1. There **is** / **are** some orange juice.

2. Sam has **some** / **three** milk.

3. We have **a** / **some** salt.

4. There **is** / **are** some apples.

5. Rita has **a** / **some** banana.

6. I've got **a** / **some** eggs.

31.3 ÉCRIVEZ CE QUE REPRÉSENTE CHAQUE IMAGE.

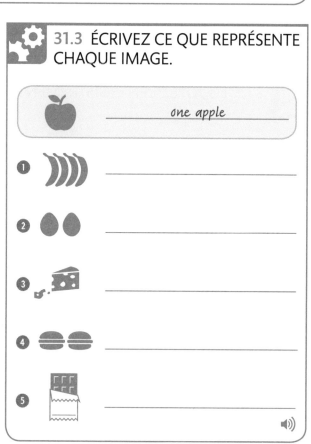

one apple

1. _____

2. _____

3. _____

4. _____

5. _____

31.4 RÉCRIVEZ LA PHRASE DE 2 MANIÈRES DIFFÉRENTES.

Are there any apples?	*There are some apples.*	*There aren't any apples.*
① Is there any salt?		
②	There is some wine.	
③ Are there any burgers?		
④	There are some cookies.	
⑤		There aren't any pastries.
⑥ Is there any bread?		
⑦	There is some rice.	
⑧		There isn't any butter.
⑨ Are there any pizzas?		
⑩	There is some cheese.	

31.5 ÉCOUTEZ L'ENREGISTREMENT, PUIS COCHEZ LES BONNES RÉPONSES.

Steve and Kate have three bags of flour.
True ☑ **False** ☐

① They have three bags of sugar in their cupboard.
True ☐ **False** ☐

② Steve and Kate haven't got any tomatoes.
True ☐ **False** ☐

③ They have two blocks of cheese.
True ☐ **False** ☐

④ Steve and Kate have got two oranges.
True ☐ **False** ☐

⑤ They haven't got any apples.
True ☐ **False** ☐

⑥ Steve and Kate don't have any coffee.
True ☐ **False** ☐

⑦ Kate doesn't have any chocolate.
True ☐ **False** ☐

⑧ Steve and Kate don't have any onions.
True ☐ **False** ☐

⑨ They have some rice.
True ☐ **False** ☐

31.6 COMPLÉTEZ LES PHRASES AVEC LES MOTS DE LA LISTE.

There is a ___*jar*___ of coffee.

④ There's a _____ of juice.

❶ There's a _____ of milk.

⑤ There are three _____ of water.

❷ There are two _____ of rice.

⑥ There's a _____ of pasta.

❸ There's a _____ of chocolate.

⑦ There are two _____ of tea.

| glass | carton | ~~jar~~ | bowl |
| cups | bar | bags | bottles |

 31.7 OBSERVEZ LES IMAGES, PUIS BARREZ LE MOT INCORRECT
DANS CHAQUE PHRASE.

There ~~is~~ / are three cartons of milk.

⑥ There isn't / aren't any bread.

❶ There is / are a jar of coffee.

❼ There is / are a bag of flour.

❷ There isn't / aren't any rice.

❽ There is / are some pasta.

❸ There is / are two cartons of juice.

❾ There is / are two bars of chocolate.

❹ There is / are some meat.

❿ There isn't / aren't any sugar.

❺ There is / are two bottles of wine.

⓫ There is / are some butter.

100

Aa 31.8 ENTOUREZ 9 RÉCIPIENTS DANS LA GRILLE.

```
K  P  D  B  O  W  L  Y  M  T
W  O  K  O  N  S  S  J  N  E
A  C  Y  T  P  S  B  O  E  E
J  Y  M  T  A  L  T  G  J  H
V  A  K  L  U  R  A  S  G  E
G  A  G  E  A  B  Z  I  B  S
R  Y  D  C  D  E  E  H  N  Q
N  W  F  G  L  D  B  Z  E  E
A  T  L  P  X  I  M  T  O  E
E  A  L  R  Y  T  K  C  S  S
R  S  C  I  D  Q  S  J  A  R
A  Q  U  Y  E  Z  D  W  T  E
N  H  P  X  O  E  C  N  N  C
K  B  T  I  B  A  R  K  D  J
Y  R  W  N  G  R  M  S  L  O
```

31.9 COMPLÉTEZ LES PHRASES AVEC « MUCH » OU « MANY ».

How __much__ rice is there?

1 How _____ meat is there?

2 How _____ cartons of milk are there?

3 How _____ bowls of rice are there?

4 How _____ juice is there?

5 How _____ bread is there?

6 How _____ cups of tea are there?

7 How _____ bars of chocolate are there?

8 How _____ coffee is there?

9 How _____ jars of jam are there?

10 How _____ milk is there?

11 How _____ bags of flour are there?

12 How _____ pizza is there?

13 How _____ eggs are there?

31.10 UTILISEZ LE SCHÉMA POUR CRÉER 6 PHRASES, PUIS LISEZ-LES À VOIX HAUTE.

How many burgers are there?

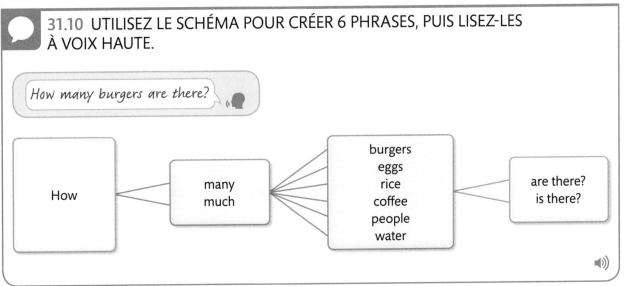

| How | many
much | burgers
eggs
rice
coffee
people
water | are there?
is there? |

32 Mesurer

Utilisez « enough » lorsque vous avez un nombre exact ou une quantité exacte. Utilisez « too many » ou « too much » pour dire « trop ».

🔧 **Grammaire** Les mesures
Aa Vocabulaire Les ingrédients et les quantités
🧩 **Compétence** Parler de quantités

 32.1 BARREZ LES MOTS INCORRECTS DANS CHAQUE PHRASE.

We have too many / ~~too much~~ eggs.

1 There are too many / too much pears.

2 There is too many / too much milk.

3 She has too many / too much pasta.

4 We have too many / too much bananas.

5 There is too many / too much butter.

6 There are too many / too much apples.

7 There are too many / too much tomatoes.

8 I have too many / too much juice.

9 There are too many / too much mushrooms.

10 They have too many / too much burgers.

11 Sue owns too many / too much shoes.

🔊

 32.2 COMPLÉTEZ LES PHRASES AVEC « IS ENOUGH » OU « ARE ENOUGH ».

There _____*is enough*_____ flour.

1 There _____ pineapples.

2 There _____ mangoes.

3 There _____ sugar.

4 There _____ bread.

5 There_____ milk.

6 There _____ pasta.

7 There _____ apples.

8 There _____ oranges.

9 There _____ bananas.

10 There _____ chocolate.

11 There _____ eggs.

12 There _____ cheese.

13 There _____ tomatoes.

14 There _____ butter.

15 There _____ juice.

🔊

32.3 RÉCRIVEZ LA PHRASE DE 2 MANIÈRES DIFFÉRENTES.

We don't have enough salt.	We have enough salt.	We have too much salt.
❶ You don't have enough oranges.		
❷	There's enough sugar.	
❸		We have too much butter.
❹	There are enough eggs.	
❺ There isn't enough flour.		
❻		There are too many potatoes.
❼	You have enough melons.	
❽ He doesn't have enough bread.		
❾		There is too much tea.
❿	We have enough milk.	
⓫ You don't have enough rice.		
⓬		There are too many mangoes.
⓭	Martha has enough onions.	
⓮ You don't have enough carrots.		

32.4 ÉCOUTEZ L'ENREGISTREMENT, PUIS COCHEZ LES BONNES RÉPONSES.

Bruce and Shelley don't have any bread.
True ☐ **False** ☑

❶ They don't have enough butter.
True ☐ **False** ☐

❷ They have too many bags of flour.
True ☐ **False** ☐

❸ They don't have enough salt.
True ☐ **False** ☐

❹ They have enough tomatoes.
True ☐ **False** ☐

❺ They don't have enough cheese.
True ☐ **False** ☐

32.5 COMPLÉTEZ LES PHRASES AVEC « ENOUGH », « NOT ENOUGH », « TOO MANY » OU « TOO MUCH ».

Vegetable pasta soup

1 onion
3 carrots
2 potatoes
4 tomatoes

15 oz pasta
3 fl oz oil
1 loaf of bread

Fruit cake

6 oz butter
9 oz flour
6 oz sugar
2 oranges

2 bananas
3 eggs
1 glass of milk

There are ___*too many*___ onions.

❶ There are _____ carrots.

❷ There are _____ potatoes.

❸ There are _____ tomatoes.

❹ There is _____ pasta.

❺ There is _____ oil.

❻ There is _____ bread.

❼ There is _____ butter.

❽ There is _____ flour.

❾ There is _____ sugar.

❿ There are _____ oranges.

⓫ There are _____ bananas.

⓬ There are _____ eggs.

⓭ There is _____ milk.

32.6 RÉCRIVEZ LES PHRASES SUIVANTES EN CORRIGEANT LES ERREURS.

There are enough corn to make the soup.
There is enough corn to make the soup.

1 There aren't enough butter.
_____

2 There isn't enough tomatoes.
_____

3 There isn't enough mangoes.
_____

4 You have too money bananas.
_____

5 They don't have enoug butter.
_____

6 There is enough onions.
_____

7 There aren't enough sugar.
_____

8 You have to many pineapples.
_____

9 They have too moch bread.
_____

10 You dont have enough apples.
_____

11 They have enogh flour.
_____

12 There is too many potatoes.
_____

13 There are too much salt.
_____

14 There are too much chocolate.
_____

15 There is too many mangoes.
_____

16 You have enugh eggs.
_____

17 There is enough oranges.
_____

🔊

32.7 UTILISEZ LE SCHÉMA POUR CRÉER 9 PHRASES, PUIS LISEZ-LES À VOIX HAUTE.

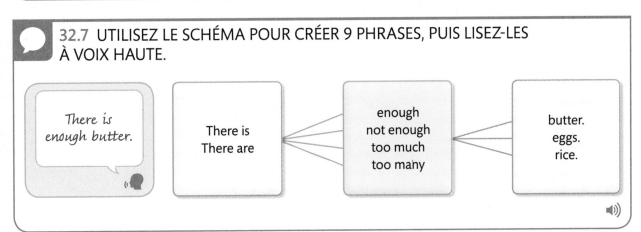

Aa 33.1 LES VÊTEMENTS, LES ACCESSOIRES ET LES COULEURS PLACEZ LES MOTS DE LA LISTE SOUS L'IMAGE CORRESPONDANTE.

blouse

❶ _____

❷ _____

❸ _____

❹ _____

❼ _____

❽ _____

❾ _____

❿ _____

⓫ _____

⓮ _____

⓯ _____

⓰ _____

⓱ _____

⓲ _____

㉑ _____

㉒ _____

㉓ _____

㉔ _____

㉕ _____

5 _____

6 _____

12 _____

13 _____

19 _____

20 _____

26 _____

27 _____

socks   extra large   red

          blue   skirt   suit

gloves   green   hat

          large   ~~blouse~~   belt

coat   black   small

          orange   jeans

          boots   sandals   scarf

shirt   medium   yellow

purple   dress   shoes

          extra small   pink

34 Dans les magasins

Plusieurs verbes sont à votre disposition pour parler de ce qui se passe lorsque vous faites des achats. Utilisez « too » et « enough » pour dire comment des vêtements vous vont.

⚙ **Grammaire** « Too » et « fit »
Aa Vocabulaire Les magasins et les vêtements
Compétence Décrire des vêtements

34.1 COMPLÉTEZ LES PHRASES AVEC LES MOTS DE LA LISTE.

Jane _____*owns*_____ a red motorcycle.

1 That sweater _____ you. It's the right size.

2 My mom always _____ my dad's clothes.

3 These jeans don't _____. They're too small.

4 I _____ 30 pairs of shoes.

5 I always _____ clothes before I buy them.

6 Those shops _____ very fashionable clothes.

7 We _____ fruit at the market.

8 I _____ some shoes for my birthday.

9 I sometimes _____ by credit card.

chooses	fits	~~owns~~	sell	pay	want	buy	fit	try on	own

🔊

34.2 RÉCRIVEZ LES PHRASES SUIVANTES EN CORRIGEANT LES ERREURS.

Sally always choose her husband's clothes.
Sally always chooses her husband's clothes.

1 Ruth do a lot of her shopping on the internet.

_____

2 The shop don't sell my size of clothes.

_____

3 She wear short skirts.

_____

4 Greg's jeans doesn't fit him.

_____

5 Amy own a lot of fashionable clothes.

_____

6 We pays for our shopping with cash.

_____

7 Duncan never try on clothes before he buys them.

_____

8 My parents usually pays for my clothes.

_____

9 Peter don't own many clothes.

_____

🔊

34.3 RÉCRIVEZ LES PHRASES SUIVANTES EN CORRIGEANT LES ERREURS.

Kim **want** a blue skirt.
Kim wants a blue skirt.

❶ That blouse **don't** fit you.

_____

❷ Sue always **try** on her new clothes.

_____

❸ Rob **want** a new tie for Christmas.

_____

❹ Peter **buy** his meat at the butcher's shop.

_____

❺ Jose **own** a beautiful house in France.

_____

❻ My jeans **doesn't** fit me. They're too big.

_____

❼ Samantha **choose** high-quality clothes.

_____

❽ They **sells** vegetables in the market.

_____

❾ Do you **wants** a new shirt for your birthday?

_____

🔊

Aa **34.4 BARREZ L'ADJECTIF INCORRECT DANS CHAQUE PHRASE.**

 This is a long / ~~short~~ dress.

❶ This is a **new** / **old** T-shirt.

❷ These are **short** / **long** jeans.

❸ This is an **cheap** / **expensive** tie.

❹ This is a **large** / **small** sweater.

❺ This is a **pink** / **blue** dress.

❻ This is an **new** / **old** T-shirt.

❼ These are **old** / **cheap** shoes.

❽ This is a **long** / **short** skirt.

❾ This is a **red** / **blue** shirt.

❿ These are **big** / **small** shoes.

⓫ This is a **large** / **small** sweater.

🔊

34.5 ÉCOUTEZ L'ENREGISTREMENT, PUIS COCHEZ LES BONNES RÉPONSES.

Jane et Ruth décrivent les vêtements qu'elles veulent acheter.

What type of cardigan does Jane buy?

red and short ☐

blue and long ☐

black and long ☑

1 What does Jane want to buy?

a red shirt ☐

a red skirt ☐

a blue skirt ☐

2 What does Ruth want to buy for her mother?

a red scarf ☐

yellow gloves ☐

a red hat ☐

3 What does Ruth want to buy?

brown shoes ☐

black shoes ☐

brown boots ☐

4 What does Jane want next?

blue jeans ☐

black jeans ☐

purple jeans ☐

5 Jane then tries on the...

black coat. ☐

red coat. ☐

green coat. ☐

Aa 34.6 ENTOUREZ 5 ADJECTIFS DANS LA GRILLE.

```
D  F  S  P  F  Q  A  T  E  H
C  E  S  T  L  S  S  T  F  Y
H  S  S  C  O  H  Y  C  Z  N
E  X  L  G  N  S  I  M  E  L
A  T  E  P  G  H  X  U  R  H
P  I  W  S  R  O  G  X  E  E
B  P  A  H  A  R  D  R  P  I
N  C  S  O  F  T  E  I  H  R
```

Aa 34.7 RELIEZ LES EXPRESSIONS AYANT LE MÊME SENS.

not big enough ———————— too expensive

1 not soft enough   too short

2 not new enough ——→ too small

3 not cheap enough   too soft

4 not short enough   too hard

5 not hard enough   too long

6 not long enough   too old

🔊

34.8 COMPLÉTEZ LES PHRASES AVEC LES MOTS DE LA LISTE, PUIS LISEZ-LES À VOIX HAUTE.

Sharon's dress is _too long_ .

1

Claire's hat is

_____ .

2

These shoes are

_____ .

3

Sophie's pullover is

_____ .

4

Corrine's coat is

_____ .

5

Emma's sweater is

_____ .

6

Chloe's scarf is

_____ .

7

Phoebe's shoes are

_____ .

8

Joshua's jacket is

_____ .

| too big | ~~too long~~ | too small | big enough | too long |
| too small | too big | too expensive | too small |

35 Décrire des choses

Vous pouvez utiliser des adjectifs pour exprimer votre opinion ou donner des précisions.
On peut mettre plusieurs adjectifs devant un nom.

⚙ **Grammaire** Les adjectifs de l'opinion
Aa Vocabulaire Les magasins et les matériaux
🧩 **Compétence** Donner votre opinion

 **35.1 LISEZ LE BLOG, PUIS COCHEZ LES BONNES RÉPONSES.**

Fashion Blog

HOME | ENTRIES | ABOUT | CONTACT

 POSTED SATURDAY, MAY 3
My next shopping trip...

Well, it's only spring, but I've got big plans about what I want to buy for the summer! I have some lovely red cotton trousers, but I want to buy some pink ones, too. I have this horrible green sweatshirt, which was a present from my friend. So I really want to buy a new sweatshirt. I want a red one!

I want some new shoes. I have some pretty yellow sandals and some sneakers, but I want to buy some heels. Leather is very trendy this year. I have a gorgeous brown leather jacket from Spain. But I want to buy some leather boots. I have lots of woolen hats for the winter. But I really want to buy a nice yellow one. I want to go to Malta in the summer, so I want to look good. Happy shopping everyone!

Jane has some red cotton trousers.
True ☑ **False** ☐

❶ Jane has a horrible blue sweatshirt.
True ☐ **False** ☐

❷ She wants a red sweatshirt.
True ☐ **False** ☐

❸ She has some yellow sandals.
True ☐ **False** ☐

❹ Jane wants some heels.
True ☐ **False** ☐

❺ She has a brown leather jacket from Greece.
True ☐ **False** ☐

❻ She wants some leather boots.
True ☐ **False** ☐

❼ She doesn't have many winter hats.
True ☐ **False** ☐

❽ She wants to buy a yellow hat.
True ☐ **False** ☐

❾ Jane wants to go to Italy this summer.
True ☐ **False** ☐

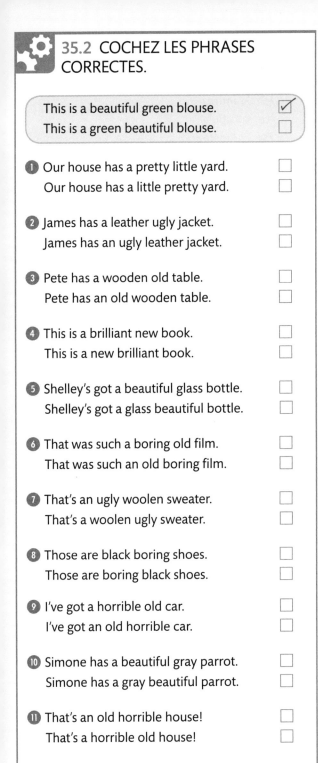

35.2 COCHEZ LES PHRASES CORRECTES.

This is a beautiful green blouse. ☑
This is a green beautiful blouse. ☐

① Our house has a pretty little yard. ☐
Our house has a little pretty yard. ☐

② James has a leather ugly jacket. ☐
James has an ugly leather jacket. ☐

③ Pete has a wooden old table. ☐
Pete has an old wooden table. ☐

④ This is a brilliant new book. ☐
This is a new brilliant book. ☐

⑤ Shelley's got a beautiful glass bottle. ☐
Shelley's got a glass beautiful bottle. ☐

⑥ That was such a boring old film. ☐
That was such an old boring film. ☐

⑦ That's an ugly woolen sweater. ☐
That's a woolen ugly sweater. ☐

⑧ Those are black boring shoes. ☐
Those are boring black shoes. ☐

⑨ I've got a horrible old car. ☐
I've got an old horrible car. ☐

⑩ Simone has a beautiful gray parrot. ☐
Simone has a gray beautiful parrot. ☐

⑪ That's an old horrible house! ☐
That's a horrible old house! ☐

⑫ You've got a red nice shirt. ☐
You've got a nice red shirt. ☐

🔊

35.3 ÉCRIVEZ LES MOTS SUIVANTS DANS LE BON ORDRE AFIN DE RECONSTITUER LES PHRASES.

| a | It's | green | hat. | lovely |

It's a lovely green hat.

① | beautiful | Jill's | got | dog. | a | black |

_____

② | new | nice | has | house. | a | Simon |

_____

③ | ugly | have | old | an | car. | They |

_____

④ | red | pretty | are | shoes. | Those |

_____

⑤ | pink | an | ugly | hat. | That's |

_____

⑥ | a | has | brown | horrible | snake. | Greg |

_____

⑦ | got | You've | black | a | bag. | beautiful |

_____

⑧ | new | is | great | a | book. | This |

_____

🔊

113

Aa 35.4 ENTOUREZ 7 MOTS DÉCRIVANT UN MATÉRIAU DANS LA GRILLE.

```
S H C G A I R C C A L C W
Q M E T A L K V O Q E V O
A E D E M J S D T K A D O
P L A S T I C G T T T I D
B T B C X W D L O X H B N
E E P A P E R A N A E D R
R M Z W O O L S R O R Z O
K S X A E B R S L S X U X
```

🎧 35.5 ÉCOUTEZ L'ENREGISTREMENT, PUIS COCHEZ LA BONNE RÉPONSE.

The shoes are...
cotton ☐ **leather** ☑ **plastic** ☐

❶ The cups are...
metal ☐ **glass** ☐ **plastic** ☐

❷ The table is...
wooden ☐ **plastic** ☐ **metal** ☐

❸ The bottle is...
plastic ☐ **glass** ☐ **metal** ☐

❹ The jacket is...
wool ☐ **leather** ☐ **plastic** ☐

❺ The chairs are...
plastic ☐ **wooden** ☐ **metal** ☐

❻ The sweater is...
wool ☐ **leather** ☐ **nylon** ☐

❼ The table is...
metal ☐ **glass** ☐ **wooden** ☐

❽ The bag is...
leather ☐ **plastic** ☐ **paper** ☐

❾ The scarf is...
wool ☐ **leather** ☐ **silk** ☐

❿ The bottle is...
glass ☐ **plastic** ☐ **metal** ☐

⓫ The bag is...
paper ☐ **plastic** ☐ **leather** ☐

⓬ The lamp is...
metal ☐ **glass** ☐ **wooden** ☐

⓭ The chairs are...
wooden ☐ **metal** ☐ **plastic** ☐

35.6 COMPLÉTEZ AVEC LES MOTS DE LA LISTE.

A broken _____*glass*_____ bottle.

4 Three _____ chairs.

1 Four _____ cups.

5 A green _____ sweater.

2 An ugly _____ table.

6 A brown _____ bag.

3 An old _____ jacket.

7 Beautiful _____.

| plastic | wooden | ~~glass~~ | paper | wool | leather | metal | fabric |

Aa 36.1 LES SPORTS PLACEZ LES MOTS DE LA LISTE SOUS L'IMAGE CORRESPONDANTE.

volleyball

1 _____

2 _____

3 _____

4 _____

5 _____

6 _____

7 _____

8 _____

9 _____

10 _____

11 _____

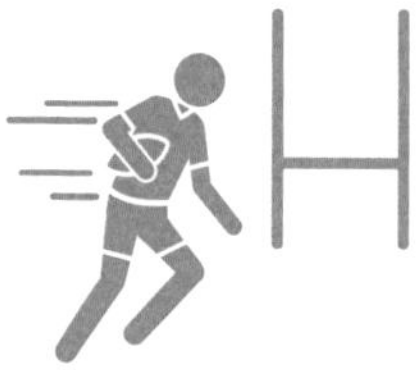

12 _____

13 _____

14 _____

15 _____

skateboarding	ice hockey	baseball	roller-skating	tennis
cycling	rugby	snowboarding	running	skiing	~~volleyball~~
basketball	swimming	badminton	golf	horse riding

36.2 LES ÉQUIPEMENTS ET LES INSTALLATIONS PLACEZ LES MOTS DE LA LISTE SOUS L'IMAGE CORRESPONDANTE.

tennis racket

① _____

② _____

③ _____

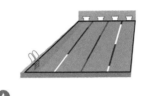

④ _____

⑤ _____

⑥ _____

⑦ _____

⑧ _____

⑨ _____

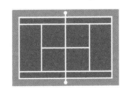

⑩ _____

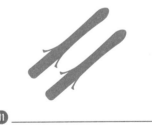

⑪ _____

surfboard	baseball bat	stadium	snowboard
swimming pool	~~tennis racket~~	tennis court	skateboard
golf club	running track	skis	golf course

37 Parler de sport

Pour parler des sports auxquels vous participez, utilisez le verbe « to go » suivi du gérondif. Pour les autres sports, utilisez « to play » suivi d'un nom.

 Grammaire « Go » et « play »

Aa Vocabulaire Les sports

Compétence Parler de sport

37.1 COMPLÉTEZ LES PHRASES SUIVANTES.

My friend Kim _____*goes running*_____ (🏃 run) three times a week in the park.

1 Douglas _____ (🚴 cycle) with his brother on Sundays.

2 Phil and John _____ (⛸ skate) in the winter.

3 Mr. Henderson _____ (⛵ sail) in the Mediterranean in the summer.

4 Veronica _____ (💃 dance) with her friends on the weekend.

5 They _____ (🥾 hike) in the mountains in Scotland.

6 Lawrence _____ (🏊 swim) on Tuesdays.

7 Ted _____ (🛹 skateboard) on Saturday morning.

8 I _____ (🐎 ride) in France each year.

9 She _____ (🛍 shop) in Milan at Christmas.

10 We _____ (🎣 fish) after work on Mondays.

11 Anne _____ (🏄 surf) in California.

37.2 BARREZ LE MOT INCORRECT DANS CHAQUE PHRASE.

We go ~~skateing~~ / skating in the park.

1. Jane goes **dancing** / **danceing** on Friday nights.

2. Our dad goes **sailing** / **saileing** in the summer.

3. I go **fisheing** / **fishing** in the evening.

4. Do you go **running** / **runing** in the morning?

5. They go **cycling** / **cycleing** in the summer.

6. Sam goes **swiming** / **swimming** on Sundays.

7. I go **horseback riding** / **horseback ridding** daily.

8. Claire goes **shopping** / **shopeing** in London.

9. Omar goes **skateboarding** / **skateboardding** daily.

10. Do you go **dancing** / **danccing** with her?

11. Rachel goes **hikking** / **hiking** in Peru.

12. I go **snowboarding** / **snowbording** in the winter.

13. Bob and Steve go **surphing** / **surfing** in Tahiti.

◀))

Aa 37.3 RÉCRIVEZ LES VERBES SUIVANTS AU GÉRONDIF.

skate	=	*skating*
1 snowboard	=	_____
2 run	=	_____
3 fish	=	_____
4 swim	=	_____
5 skateboard	=	_____
6 dance	=	_____
7 surf	=	_____
8 shop	=	_____
9 cycle	=	_____
10 sail	=	_____
11 ride	=	_____

◀))

37.4 COMPLÉTEZ LES PHRASES AVEC « GO » OU « GOES », PUIS LISEZ-LES À VOIX HAUTE.

Sal __goes__ sailing at the lake.

1. I _____ shopping in the evening.

2. Jan _____ skateboarding on Fridays.

3. Pete _____ sailing on the weekend.

4. Sam _____ skating every December.

5. I _____ running on Wednesday.

6. They _____ fishing with their friends.

7. Sarah _____ dancing on Saturdays.

◀))

37.5 BARREZ LE MOT INCORRECT DANS CHAQUE PHRASE.

He ~~play~~ / **plays** baseball on Sundays.

1 Do you **play** / **plays** chess?

2 Paolo **play** / **plays** badminton at the weekend.

3 My father **play** / **plays** golf with his friends.

4 We **don't play** / **doesn't play** baseball anymore.

5 I **play** / **plays** tennis with my brother.

6 Greg **don't play** / **doesn't play** basketball.

7 Liz **play** / **plays** racquet ball on the weekend.

8 Your dad **don't play** / **doesn't play** soccer.

9 Our dog **plays** / **play** with its ball.

10 Mike **play** / **plays** soccer on Saturdays.

11 We **don't play** / **doesn't play** golf in the winter.

12 Pammy **don't play** / **doesn't play** tennis.

37.6 RÉCRIVEZ LES PHRASES À LA FORME INTERROGATIVE.

They play soccer on weekends.
Do they play soccer on weekends?

1 He plays badminton on Fridays.

_____

2 Noah plays golf with his grandpa.

_____

3 They play basketball with their friends.

_____

4 Georgia plays baseball at school.

_____

5 We play tennis in the summer.

_____

6 Tim's parents play chess in the evening.

_____

37.7 ÉCOUTEZ L'ENREGISTREMENT, PUIS COCHEZ LA BONNE RÉPONSE.

Mark doesn't play golf during the week.
True ☑ **False** ☐

1 Steven goes cycling in the winter.
True ☐ **False** ☐

2 Max goes running every evening.
True ☐ **False** ☐

3 Ian plays soccer four times a week.
True ☐ **False** ☐

4 Janine hates running.
True ☐ **False** ☐

5 Lila goes skating with her sister.
True ☐ **False** ☐

6 Robbie doesn't go running anymore.
True ☐ **False** ☐

7 Susan goes fishing on the weekend.
True ☐ **False** ☐

37.8 COMPLÉTEZ LES PHRASES EN UTILISANT « GO », « GOES », « PLAY » OU « PLAYS ».

They _____*go*_____ running every week.

① John _____ badminton on Wednesday.

② You _____ fishing with your brother.

③ My uncle _____ chess with my aunt.

④ We _____ dancing in the evening.

⑤ Sally's dad _____ rugby.

⑥ Bartou _____ cycling in the mountains.

⑦ Ramona _____ racquet ball with her dad.

⑧ Our kids _____ baseball after school.

⑨ Simon and Pam _____ surfing in the summer.

⑩ They _____ basketball every Saturday.

⑪ We _____ snowboarding in Austria.

37.9 À L'AIDE DES IMAGES, COMPLÉTEZ LES PHRASES, PUIS LISEZ-LES À VOIX HAUTE.

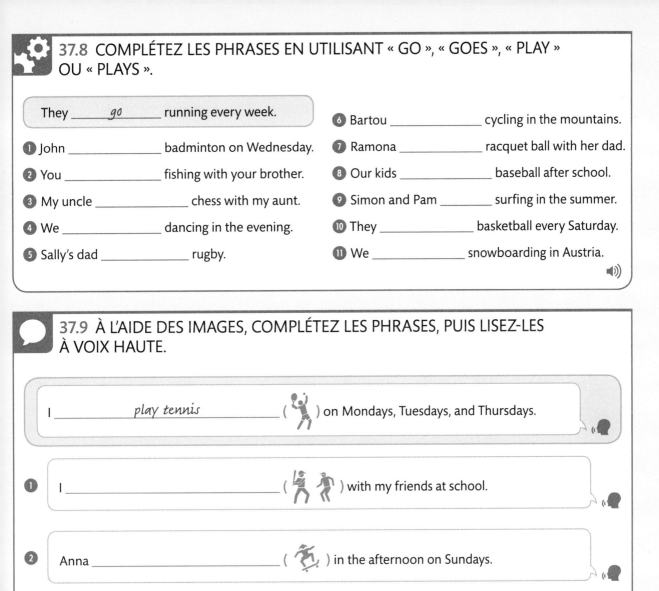

I _____ *play tennis* _____ ( ) on Mondays, Tuesdays, and Thursdays.

① I _____ ( ) with my friends at school.

② Anna _____ ( ) in the afternoon on Sundays.

③ Mrs. Amir _____ ( ) with her husband in the evening.

④ Max _____ ( ) on Tuesdays and Fridays.

⑤ Peter _____ ( ) with his brother on Mondays and Wednesdays.

121

38 Vocabulaire

Aa 38.1 **LES LOISIRS ET LES PASSE-TEMPS** PLACEZ LES ACTIVITÉS DE LA LISTE SOUS L'IMAGE CORRESPONDANTE.

cook

❶ _____

❷ _____

❸ _____

❹ _____

❺ _____

❼ _____

❽ _____

❾ _____

❿ _____

⓫ _____

⓮ _____

⓯ _____

⓰ _____

⓱ _____

⓲ _____

㉑ _____

㉒ _____

㉓ _____

㉔ _____

㉕ _____

5 _____

6 _____

12 _____

13 _____

19 _____

20 _____

26 _____

27 _____

play cards   paint   sew

go camping   write   take photos

go out for a meal   visit a museum

~~cook~~   watch television   play chess

go shopping   read   do yoga

watch a movie   play a musical instrument

go to the gym   bake   see a play

play video games   walk / hike

meet friends   do the gardening

draw   go bird watching   knit

do puzzles   listen to music

39 Parler de votre temps libre

Les adverbes de fréquence permettent d'indiquer la fréquence à laquelle vous effectuez une activité. On place généralement l'adverbe entre le sujet et le verbe.

⚙️ **Grammaire** Les adverbes de fréquence
Aa Vocabulaire Les passe-temps
🧩 **Compétence** Parler de votre temps libre

39.1 LISEZ LE COURRIEL, PUIS COCHEZ LES BONNES RÉPONSES.

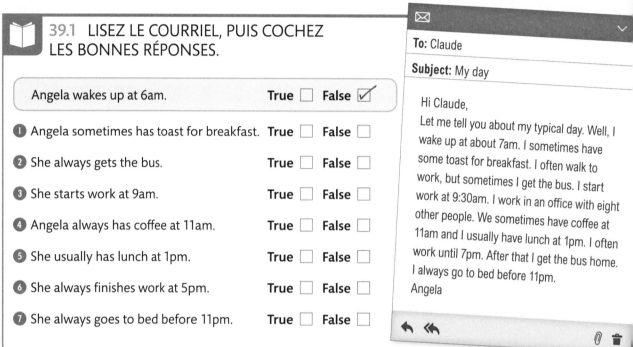

Angela wakes up at 6am. **True** ☐ **False** ☑

1 Angela sometimes has toast for breakfast. **True** ☐ **False** ☐

2 She always gets the bus. **True** ☐ **False** ☐

3 She starts work at 9am. **True** ☐ **False** ☐

4 Angela always has coffee at 11am. **True** ☐ **False** ☐

5 She usually has lunch at 1pm. **True** ☐ **False** ☐

6 She always finishes work at 5pm. **True** ☐ **False** ☐

7 She always goes to bed before 11pm. **True** ☐ **False** ☐

✉️

To: Claude

Subject: My day

Hi Claude,
Let me tell you about my typical day. Well, I wake up at about 7am. I sometimes have some toast for breakfast. I often walk to work, but sometimes I get the bus. I start work at 9:30am. I work in an office with eight other people. We sometimes have coffee at 11am and I usually have lunch at 1pm. I often work until 7pm. After that I get the bus home. I always go to bed before 11pm.
Angela

39.2 ÉCRIVEZ LES MOTS SUIVANTS DANS LE BON ORDRE AFIN DE RECONSTITUER LES PHRASES.

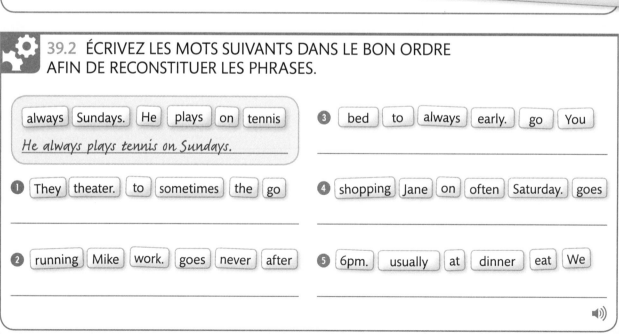

always Sundays. He plays on tennis

He always plays tennis on Sundays.

1 They theater. to sometimes the go

_____

2 running Mike work. goes never after

_____

3 bed to always early. go You

_____

4 shopping Jane on often Saturday. goes

_____

5 6pm. usually at dinner eat We

_____

How often does John go running?

always ☐
usually ☑
sometimes ☐

1 How often does Chris get up early?

never ☐
sometimes ☐
often ☐

2 How often does Shelley go swimming?

never ☐
sometimes ☐
usually ☐

3 How often does Flo have tea in the morning?

sometimes ☐
often ☐
always ☐

4 How often does Sylvester go to bed at 10pm?

often ☐
usually ☐
always ☐

5 How often does Dominic play soccer?

never ☐
usually ☐
always ☐

6 How often does David read a newspaper?

sometimes ☐
often ☐
always ☐

I get up early. [rarely]

I rarely get up early.

1 Clara plays chess with her grandfather. [never]

2 Enzo eats chocolate ice cream. [always]

3 Paul goes fishing in the morning. [sometimes]

4 My parents drive to work. [usually]

5 Gill goes shopping with her mom. [never]

6 You go to the gym in the town. [sometimes]

7 Shelley watches TV in the evening. [usually]

8 My dog sleeps under the table. [always]

9 We play baseball in the summer. [sometimes]

10 Tim rides his horse on the weekend. [usually]

39.5 ÉCRIVEZ LES MOTS SUIVANTS DANS LE BON ORDRE AFIN DE RECONSTITUER LES PHRASES.

finish | does | When | work? | Claudia

When does Claudia finish work?

4 you | to | When | do | go | usually | bed?

_____

1 Steph | does | TV? | watch | often | How

_____

5 May | often | How | does | running? | go

_____

2 visit | your | dad? | often | you | do | How

_____

6 play | do | How | you | tennis? | often

_____

3 play | do | soccer? | they | When

_____

7 does | Jo | How | read | a | book? | often

_____

39.6 RÉPONDEZ AUX QUESTIONS SUIVANTES.

When does he go running?

_____*He goes running*_____ on Sundays.

1 When does Kelly go to the gym?

_____ on Wednesdays.

2 When does Pete play soccer?

_____ in the evening.

3 How often does Angie go to the theater?

She never _____ .

4 How often does Jake read a newspaper?

He sometimes _____ .

5 How often does she visit her family?

_____ four times a year.

6 When does Ben play baseball?

_____ every afternoon.

7 How often does Marion go shopping?

_____ twice a week.

8 When do you read a book?

_____ every evening.

9 How often does Pam make a cake?

She sometimes _____ .

39.7 RÉCRIVEZ CHAQUE AFFIRMATION À LA FORME INTERROGATIVE EN UTILISANT « HOW OFTEN ».

She goes dancing every Friday.
How often does she go dancing?

1 Jimmy plays soccer once a week.

2 I phone my grandma twice a day.

3 Sheila gets up at 7am every day.

4 I read a book every evening in bed.

5 Sally goes to work every day.

6 I play badminton once a week.

7 My daughter goes running every evening.

8 Megan goes fishing twice a month.

9 I watch TV every evening.

39.8 COMPLÉTEZ LES PHRASES AVEC LES MOTS DE LA LISTE, PUIS LISEZ-LES À VOIX HAUTE.

Helen sometimes ___*goes*___ to the gym.

1 She always _____ dancing on the weekend.

2 I often _____ fishing.

3 My mom never _____ early.

4 Seb usually _____ soccer on weekends.

5 Tracy never _____ TV in the evening.

6 We sometimes _____ the bus to work.

7 Doug often _____ tennis on Fridays.

plays   take   go   gets up   goes   watches   plays   ~~goes~~

127

40

Exprimer vos goûts

Les verbes « to love », « to like » et « to hate » vous permettent d'exprimer ce que vous ressentez.
Vous pouvez les utiliser avec un nom ou un gérondif.

⚙ **Grammaire** « Love », « like » et « hate »

Aa **Vocabulaire** La nourriture, les sports et les passe-temps

🧩 **Compétence** Parler de ce que vous aimez

Aa 40.1 RELIEZ CHAQUE IMAGE À LA PHRASE CORRESPONDANTE.

We love basketball.

Bill doesn't like cats.

We like cake.

I hate tennis.

Samantha likes chocolate.

I don't like pasta.

They hate board games.

Shelley loves pizza.

🔊

🎧 40.2 ÉCOUTEZ L'ENREGISTREMENT, PUIS COCHEZ LA BONNE RÉPONSE.

What does Doug like?
fruits ☐ fast food ☑

❶ What does Doug hate?
salad ☐ fries ☐

❷ What does Shelley love?
sports ☐ painting ☐

❸ What does she like doing on the weekend?
playing tennis ☐ reading books ☐

❹ What does she not like?
tennis ☐ golf ☐

❺ What does Doug love doing?
watching TV ☐ listening to music ☐

❻ What music does Doug like?
pop music ☐ classical music ☐

❼ What does he dislike doing?
going shopping ☐ reading newspapers ☐

❽ What does Shelley like doing in her free time?
cooking ☐ going to the cinema ☐

❾ What does Shelley dislike?
cooking ☐ scary films ☐

❿ What does she like doing?
taking photos ☐ visiting museums ☐

40.3 RÉCRIVEZ LES PHRASES À LA FORME NÉGATIVE.

Jack likes London.	Jack doesn't like London.
① Chris likes spiders.	
② They love Paris.	
③ Mrs. McGregor likes cats.	
④ We love soccer.	
⑤ We like wine.	
⑥ Simone loves her horse.	
⑦ He likes your necklace.	
⑧ Jean-Marie loves sports.	
⑨ Colin likes pizza.	
⑩ Douglas likes Anne.	
⑪ Cynthia hates dogs.	
⑫ We love chocolate.	
⑬ You like cheese.	
⑭ Susan likes pizza.	

40.4 UTILISEZ LE SCHÉMA POUR CRÉER 12 PHRASES, PUIS LISEZ-LES À VOIX HAUTE.

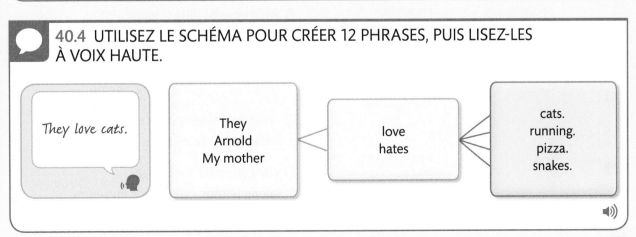

40.5 LISEZ LE BLOG, PUIS RÉPONDEZ AUX QUESTIONS.

> What is Jane's job?
>
> _She's a doctor._

1 What does she like doing in her free time?

_____

2 What is her favorite food?

_____

3 What does Jane not like cooking?

_____

4 What does she do on the weekend?

_____

5 What food does she not like?

_____

6 What does Jane hate?

_____

Lifestyle

HOME | ENTRIES | ABOUT | CONTACT

POSTED WEDNESDAY, MARCH 23

Jane's world

I'm Jane Petersen and I write this blog.
So, what about me? Well, I'm 29 years old and come from New York. I'm a doctor, but I love cooking in my free time…

My grandmother is from Italy, so I like cooking Italian food. It's my favorite. I'm a vegetarian, so I don't like cooking meat. But I love cooking fish. On weekends I love cooking for my friends and family. What else? In my free time I like jogging, and going to the gym with my friends. What do I not like? Well, I don't like fast food. Oh, and I hate candy!

I hope you enjoy my blog!

40.6 COMPLÉTEZ LES PHRASES EN UTILISANT LA FORME AFFIRMATIVE OU NÉGATIVE DES VERBES ENTRE PARENTHÈSES.

> Claire _does not like_ (not like) swimming, but she _loves_ (love) playing tennis.

1 I _____ (hate) cities, but I _____ (love) the country.

2 Archie _____ (like) ice cream, and he _____ (love) pizza.

3 He _____ (love) meat, but he _____ (hate) fish.

4 Francis _____ (not like) coffee, but he _____ (like) tea.

5 We _____ (hate) Mondays, but we _____ (love) Fridays.

6 My dad _____ (dislike) classical music, but he _____ (love) rock.

40.7 RELIEZ CHAQUE DÉBUT DE PHRASE À LA FIN CORRESPONDANTE.

I hate cheese.

She thinks it's delicious.

1 Sam likes watching soccer

because she is a vegetarian.

2 Marie loves pizza.

because it is tiring.

3 I love reading history books

I think it's disgusting.

4 Sally doesn't like running

because he doesn't have a sweet tooth.

5 Peggy does not like eating meat

because they're really interesting.

6 Paolo does not eat chocolate

She thinks they are scary.

7 Jemma hates snakes.

because it's exciting.

40.8 LISEZ LE COURRIEL, PUIS COCHEZ LES BONNES RÉPONSES.

The cafés and bars by the sea are...
boring ☐ **exciting** ☑ **interesting.** ☐

1 The weather in Sardinia is...
hot ☐ **cold** ☐ **rainy.** ☐

2 The museum in the town is really...
exciting ☐ **interesting** ☐ **tiring.** ☐

3 Si loves pizza because it is...
disgusting ☐ **tiring** ☐ **delicious.** ☐

4 Samantha hates pasta because it is...
interesting ☐ **boring** ☐ **delicious.** ☐

5 Si doesn't like walking because it's...
exciting ☐ **tiring** ☐ **boring.** ☐

To: Charles

Subject: Italy trip

Hi Charles,
We're in Sardinia on holiday. It's very hot here. There are some great cafés and bars by the ocean. They're really exciting in the evening. There's also an interesting museum in the town. I like it a lot, and there are lots of exhibits.
The food here is amazing. I love the pizza here. It's delicious. Samantha hates the pasta, though. She thinks it's really boring!
In the afternoons we go walking. Samantha loves it, but I don't! I really hate it because it's so tiring.

Hope you're all well,
Si

41 Vocabulaire

Aa 41.1 **LA MUSIQUE** PLACEZ LES MOTS DE LA LISTE SOUS L'IMAGE CORRESPONDANT

band

1 _____

2 _____

3 _____

7 _____

8 _____

9 _____

10 _____

14 _____

15 _____

16 _____

17 _____

21 _____

22 _____

23 _____

24 _____

4 _____

5 _____

6 _____

11 _____

12 _____

13 _____

18 _____

19 _____

20 _____

25 _____

26 _____

27 _____

guitar player   orchestra

headphones   Latin

flute   sing a song

~~band~~   rap   drum

rock   saxophone   trumpet

play the trumpet   violin

dance   piano

concert   microphone

conductor   keyboard

harmonica   jazz

audience   country

album   electric guitar

opera   guitar

42 Exprimer vos préférences

On utilise « like » et « love » pour indiquer à quel point on apprécie quelque chose. On utilise « favorite » pour désigner l'élément que l'on aime le plus dans un groupe.

Grammaire Utiliser « favorite »
Aa Vocabulaire La nourriture et la musique
Compétence Parler de ce que vous préférez

42.1 COCHEZ LA DESCRIPTION QUI CORRESPOND À CHAQUE IMAGE.

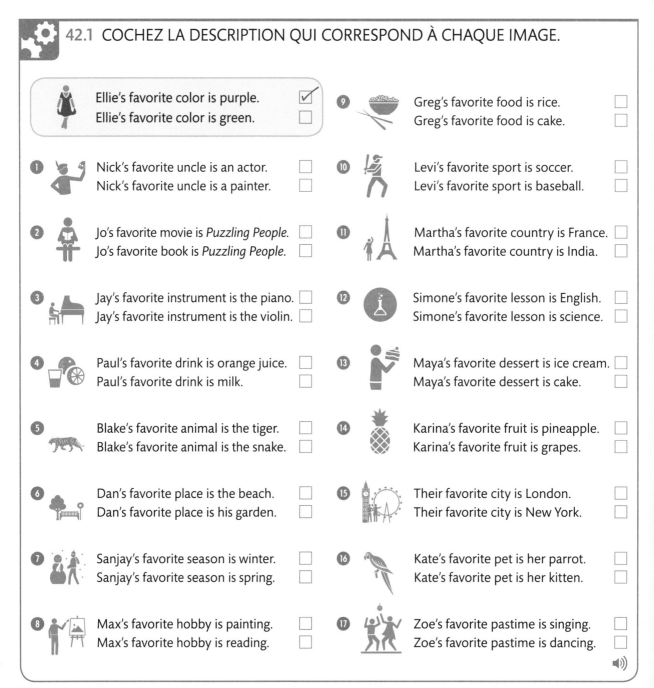

Ellie's favorite color is purple. ✓
Ellie's favorite color is green. ☐

① Nick's favorite uncle is an actor. ☐
Nick's favorite uncle is a painter. ☐

② Jo's favorite movie is *Puzzling People*. ☐
Jo's favorite book is *Puzzling People*. ☐

③ Jay's favorite instrument is the piano. ☐
Jay's favorite instrument is the violin. ☐

④ Paul's favorite drink is orange juice. ☐
Paul's favorite drink is milk. ☐

⑤ Blake's favorite animal is the tiger. ☐
Blake's favorite animal is the snake. ☐

⑥ Dan's favorite place is the beach. ☐
Dan's favorite place is his garden. ☐

⑦ Sanjay's favorite season is winter. ☐
Sanjay's favorite season is spring. ☐

⑧ Max's favorite hobby is painting. ☐
Max's favorite hobby is reading. ☐

⑨ Greg's favorite food is rice. ☐
Greg's favorite food is cake. ☐

⑩ Levi's favorite sport is soccer. ☐
Levi's favorite sport is baseball. ☐

⑪ Martha's favorite country is France. ☐
Martha's favorite country is India. ☐

⑫ Simone's favorite lesson is English. ☐
Simone's favorite lesson is science. ☐

⑬ Maya's favorite dessert is ice cream. ☐
Maya's favorite dessert is cake. ☐

⑭ Karina's favorite fruit is pineapple. ☐
Karina's favorite fruit is grapes. ☐

⑮ Their favorite city is London. ☐
Their favorite city is New York. ☐

⑯ Kate's favorite pet is her parrot. ☐
Kate's favorite pet is her kitten. ☐

⑰ Zoe's favorite pastime is singing. ☐
Zoe's favorite pastime is dancing. ☐

🔊

42.2 ÉCOUTEZ L'ENREGISTREMENT, PUIS COCHEZ LA BONNE RÉPONSE.

Quelques personnes évoquent leurs préférences.

Dave's favorite type of music in the morning is... **soul** ☐ **jazz** ☑ **rock.** ☐

1 Jenny's favorite subject at school is... **physics** ☐ **math** ☐ **biology.** ☐

2 Mike's favorite day of the week is... **Monday** ☐ **Wednesday** ☐ **Friday.** ☐

3 Colin's favorite color is... **red** ☐ **yellow** ☐ **purple.** ☐

4 Sally's favorite dessert is... **ice cream** ☐ **chocolate cake** ☐ **apple pie.** ☐

5 Danny's favorite sport is... **soccer** ☐ **basketball** ☐ **baseball.** ☐

6 Clarice's favorite season is... **summer** ☐ **fall** ☐ **winter.** ☐

42.3 RÉCRIVEZ LES PHRASES SUIVANTES EN CORRIGEANT LES ERREURS.

Her love type of music is rock.
Her favorite type of music is rock.

1 Barbara likes listen to music in the evening.

_____

2 Arnold favorite food is ice cream and pizza.

_____

3 Craig don't like getting up in the morning.

_____

4 Seb's favorite type music is hip-hop.

_____

5 Ruth like orange juice.

_____

6 Daniel favorite animal is the lion.

_____

7 I likes bacon and eggs for breakfast.

_____

8 Aziz don't like lasagna or spaghetti.

_____

9 Miguel love going to the movie theater.

_____

42.4 LISEZ LE COURRIEL, PUIS COCHEZ LES BONNES RÉPONSES.

To: Ben

Subject: My town

Hi Ben,

Netherton is small, very small. Only 800 people live here, but there's lots to do. In the morning, a lot of people take their dogs for a walk. Some people like to go to the park, but the favorite place is by the river. It's beautiful. Drinking coffee is popular here. Some people go to Dino's café, and there's a café in the supermarket. But the favorite place is Alfredo's. It's always very busy in the morning.

Dino's café is very popular at lunchtime, though, because they serve delicious pizzas there. It's the favorite place for lunch. There's a French restaurant called Chez Jean-Claude, but it's very expensive.

There's a swimming pool and a tennis court. The tennis court is the favorite place for young people to go in the summer. In the winter everyone likes to go to the swimming pool.

In the evening, there isn't much to do. There is one bar and a nightclub, but people don't like to go there. A lot of people go to the nearest city of Silchester on weekends. There are lots of nightclubs there.

Norah

Netherton is a small town.	**True** ☑	**False** ☐

❶ A lot of people walk their dogs in Netherton.	**True** ☐	**False** ☐
❷ The park is people's favorite place to walk their dogs.	**True** ☐	**False** ☐
❸ Alfredo's is always empty in the mornings.	**True** ☐	**False** ☐
❹ Dino's café is people's favorite place to drink coffee.	**True** ☐	**False** ☐
❺ Dino's is the favorite place to eat lunch.	**True** ☐	**False** ☐
❻ Chez Jean-Claude is a cheap restaurant.	**True** ☐	**False** ☐
❼ People go to the tennis court in the winter.	**True** ☐	**False** ☐
❽ The bar and disco are not very popular.	**True** ☐	**False** ☐
❾ People go to the city on weekends.	**True** ☐	**False** ☐
❿ There are lots of nightclubs in Silchester.	**True** ☐	**False** ☐

42.5 COMPLÉTEZ LES PHRASES AVEC LES MOTS DE LA LISTE CORRESPONDANTS.

 Liz's favorite fruit is an _____ *apple* _____.

spaghetti

① Arnie's favorite sport is _____ .

Chris Minota

② Joan's favorite animal is a _____ .

tennis

③ Hassan's favorite actor is _____ .

~~apple~~

④ Pam's favorite number is _____ .

strawberry

⑤ Jane's favorite sport is _____ .

dolphin

⑥ Dora's favorite ice cream is _____ .

21

⑦ Jim's favorite food is _____ .

badminton

🔊

42.6 UTILISEZ LE SCHÉMA POUR CRÉER 14 PHRASES, PUIS LISEZ-LES À VOIX HAUTE.

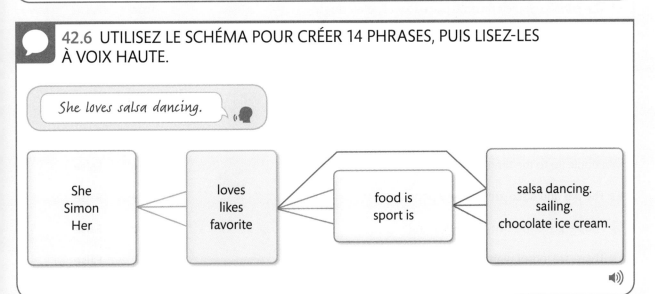

She loves salsa dancing.

137

Vocabulaire

Aa 43.1 **LES COMPÉTENCES** PLACEZ LES MOTS DE LA LISTE SOUS L'IMAGE CORRESPONDANTE.

whisper

1 _____

2 _____

3 _____

7 _____

8 _____

9 _____

10 _____

14 _____

15 _____

16 _____

17 _____

21 _____

22 _____

23 _____

24 _____

4 _____

5 _____

6 _____

11 _____

12 _____

13 _____

18 _____

19 _____

20 _____

25 _____

26 _____

27 _____

act	lift
drive	catch
work	jump
~~whisper~~	listen
sit	understand
subtract	fly
kick	climb
shout	spell
make (a snowman)	
add	throw
move	hit
carry	see
stand up	walk
talk	ride
do (homework)	

44 Ce que vous pouvez ou ne pouvez pas faire

Utilisez « can » pour parler de choses que vous êtes capable de faire, comme faire du vélo ou jouer de la guitare. Utilisez « cannot » ou « can't » pour parler de ce que vous ne pouvez pas faire.

⚙ **Grammaire** « Can », « cannot » et « can't »

Aa Vocabulaire Les talents et les compétences

🧩 **Compétence** Dire ce que vous pouvez ou ne pouvez pas faire

 44.1 RÉCRIVEZ LA PHRASE DE 2 MANIÈRES DIFFÉRENTES.

I can read Russian.	I cannot read Russian.	I can't read Russian.
❶ _____	I cannot ride a horse.	_____
❷ I can climb a tree.	_____	_____
❸ _____	_____	I can't speak French.
❹ _____	I cannot sing.	_____
❺ _____	_____	I can't lift a box.
❻ _____	I cannot fly a kite.	_____
❼ I can catch a fish.	_____	_____
❽ _____	I cannot swim.	_____

44.2 RÉCRIVEZ LES PHRASES SUIVANTES EN CORRIGEANT LES ERREURS.

Ben **can't to cook** paella.
Ben can't cook paella.

❶ Kate **can hitting** the ball.
_____

❷ Paul **can't to do** math.
_____

❸ Helen **can to spell** very well.
_____

❹ Ivan **can't running** very fast.
_____

❺ Sara **can to move** the chair.
_____

❻ Alex **can't to play** badminton.
_____

❼ Lynn **can riding** a bicycle.
_____

🔊

44.3 ÉCRIVEZ LES MOTS SUIVANTS DANS LE BON ORDRE AFIN DE RECONSTITUER LES PHRASES.

that | chair. | can | Sylvia | carry

Sylvia can carry that chair.

4 stick. | can | a | Mick | throw

_____

1 drive | car. | Eliza | cannot | a

_____

5 math. | can't | Laura | do

_____

2 piano. | Jonathan | play | can | the

_____

6 lift | can | the | Alan | box.

_____

3 jump | very | can't | high. | Cathy

_____

7 far. | very | can't | Julia | swim

_____

44.4 INA PEUT-ELLE FAIRE L'ACTIVITÉ DÉCRITE OU PAS ? ÉCOUTEZ L'ENREGISTREMENT, PUIS COCHEZ LA BONNE RÉPONSE.

Can ☐ Can't ☑

1 Can ☐ Can't ☐

2 Can ☐ Can't ☐

3 Can ☐ Can't ☐

4 Can ☐ Can't ☐

5 Can ☐ Can't ☐

44.5 POSEZ DES QUESTIONS À PARTIR DES PHRASES SUIVANTES.

Paul and Mary can speak Russian.
Can Paul and Mary speak Russian?

1 Maria and Juan can spell English words.

_____

2 The children can't do their math homework.

_____

3 I can't sing difficult jazz songs.

_____

4 Mark can't ride a horse.

_____

5 Jack can climb a tree.

_____

6 He can't carry that box. It's too heavy.

_____

7 Carlos can kick a football.

_____

8 Adam and Ella can dance the tango.

_____

9 Peter and John can't swim.

_____

 44.6 COMPLÉTEZ LES PHRASES EN UTILISANT LES MOTS DE LA LISTE.

Janet is a chef at a five star restaurant. She can _____ _cook very well_ _____ .

1 Jack is a diving teacher. He can _____ .

2 Carla lives on a farm. She can _____ and look after animals.

3 Bobby is good at languages. He can _____ .

4 Nuna likes going on winter vacations. She can _____ .

5 Jim is a great children's teacher. He can _____ well.

speak Russian   ~~cook very well~~   ski well   tell stories   swim very well   ride a horse

142

44.7 RÉPONDEZ AUX QUESTIONS SUIVANTES, PUIS LISEZ VOS RÉPONSES À VOIX HAUTE.

Can you lift a heavy box?

Yes, *I can.*

1 Can you jump over the wall?

Yes, _____

2 Can you catch that big fish?

No, _____

3 Can you throw a stick for the dog?

Yes, _____

4 Can you speak Italian?

No, _____

5 Can you play the violin?

No, _____

6 Can you climb that tree?

Yes, _____

7 Can you do Sudoku puzzles?

No, _____

8 Can you sing?

No, _____

9 Can you ride a bicycle?

No, _____

10 Can you move the kitchen table?

Yes, _____

11 Can you cook roast chicken?

Yes, _____

44.8 UTILISEZ LE SCHÉMA POUR CRÉER 18 PHRASES, PUIS LISEZ-LES À VOIX HAUTE.

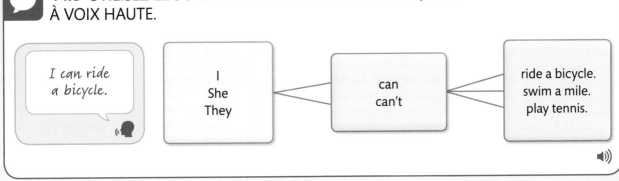

I can ride a bicycle.

| I She They | can can't | ride a bicycle. swim a mile. play tennis. |

45 Décrire vos actions

Les mots « quietly » et « loudly » sont des adverbes.
Ils permettent de donner plus d'informations concernant
le verbe. Vous pouvez donc les utiliser pour décrire
la façon dont vous faites quelque chose.

🔧 **Grammaire** Les adverbes réguliers et irréguliers
Aa Vocabulaire Les loisirs et les activités
🧩 **Compétence** Décrire des activités

45.1 COMPLÉTEZ LES PHRASES AVEC LES ADVERBES DE LA LISTE.

Sanjay plays the guitar ___*badly*___ .

3 Alan can speak German _____ .

1 My friend speaks too _____ .

4 My dog can run very _____ .

2 A turtle walks very _____ .

5 I get up very _____ .

| early | well | quietly | slowly | fast | ~~badly~~ |

🔊

45.2 RÉCRIVEZ CHACUNE DES PHRASES EN VOUS AIDANT DE L'EXEMPLE.

| Sally speaks Japanese well. | *Sally's good at speaking Japanese.* |

1 Patrick dances well. _____

2 _____ Caitlin is good at baking.

3 My mother writes well. _____

4 _____ Ethan is good at playing the guitar.

5 Aimee skis well. _____

6 _____ They are good at swimming.

7 We speak English well. _____

8 _____ Lara is good at climbing trees.

45.3 RÉCRIVEZ LES PHRASES SUIVANTES EN CORRIGEANT LES ERREURS.

My sister dances very good.
My sister dances very well.

1 Haruda sometimes arrives lately for school.

_____

2 My cousin Paul runs quick.

_____

3 Shelley sings beautiful.

_____

4 Our neighbors talk so noisy at night.

_____

5 Rosa reads very slow.

_____

6 I can pass this exam easy.

_____

7 My aunt drives very careful.

_____

8 Anita works very hardly.

_____

9 We usual go to bed at 11pm.

_____

10 Angela speaks English bad.

_____

11 A cheetah runs very fastly.

_____

12 Sarah eats her food very quick.

_____

13 Andrew does his homework good.

_____

45.4 UTILISEZ LE SCHÉMA POUR CRÉER 18 PHRASES, PUIS LISEZ-LES À VOIX HAUTE.

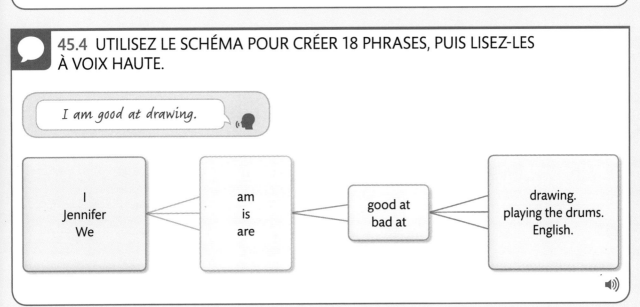

I am good at drawing.

| I / Jennifer / We | am / is / are | good at / bad at | drawing. / playing the drums. / English. |

46 Décrire vos compétences

Les mots « quite » et « very » sont des adverbes modificateurs. Vous pouvez les utiliser devant d'autres adverbes pour préciser la façon dont vous faites quelque chose.

⚙ **Grammaire** Les adverbes modificateurs
Aa Vocabulaire Les aptitudes et compétences
🧩 **Compétence** Parler de ce que vous faites bien

46.1 COCHEZ LES PHRASES CORRECTES.

Your cousin at skiing is very good. ☐
Your cousin is very good at skiing. ☑

1 Pedro is really good at history. ☐
   Pedro really good is at history. ☐

2 You speak really well French. ☐
   You speak French really well. ☐

3 Sandra is very good at singing. ☐
   Sandra very good is at singing. ☐

4 Sal is at skiing quite good. ☐
   Sal is quite good at skiing. ☐

5 Very well your uncle can swim. ☐
   Your uncle can swim very well. ☐

6 They quite fast can run. ☐
   They can run quite fast. ☐

7 Mr. Henderson is really good at golf. ☐
   At golf Mr. Henderson is really good. ☐

🔊

46.2 ÉCRIVEZ LES MOTS SUIVANTS DANS LE BON ORDRE AFIN DE RECONSTITUER LES PHRASES.

| quite | soccer. | good at | is | playing | Tim |

Tim is quite good at playing soccer.

1 | isn't | at | very | art and design. | good | Arnold |

_____

2 | is | English. | speaking | really | cousin | good | at | My |

_____

3 | is | at | climbing | Jean | quite | mountains. | good |

_____

🔊

46.3 COMPLÉTEZ LES PHRASES SUIVANTES AVEC « WELL » OU « GOOD AT ».

| Sam and Pauline are very good at singing. | *Sam and Pauline sing very well.* |

1. _____ | My aunt speaks Polish quite well.
2. Your brother is really good at surfing. | _____
3. Katie is very good at painting. | _____
4. _____ | Silvia sings really well.
5. _____ | Martina dances very well.
6. Serge is quite good at cooking. | _____
7. _____ | Sonia plays chess really well.
8. Ricky is very good at running. | _____
9. _____ | Peter draws quite well.
10. My mom is really good at speaking Greek. | _____
11. _____ | David plays the drums very well.

46.4 RÉCRIVEZ LES PHRASES SUIVANTES EN PLAÇANT LES ADVERBES AU BON ENDROIT, PUIS LISEZ-LES À VOIX HAUTE.

My brother can run fast. [very]

My brother can run very fast.

1. Charlotte can ski well. [quite]

2. Harry sings quietly. [really]

3. My aunt walks slowly. [very]

4. Elizabeth speaks Russian well. [very]

5. My dog can jump high. [quite]

6. William speaks Japanese badly. [really]

7. Philip eats noisily. [quite]

47 Exprimer vos souhaits

Vous pouvez utiliser « I want » et « I would like » pour indiquer ce que vous voulez faire. Vous pouvez aussi les utiliser à la forme négative pour dire ce que vous ne désirez pas faire.

⚙ **Grammaire** « Would » et « want »
Aa Vocabulaire Les activités de loisir
🧩 **Compétence** Parler de vos ambitions

 47.1 RÉCRIVEZ LES PHRASES SUIVANTES DE 2 MANIÈRES DIFFÉRENTES.

I want to buy a house.	I would like to buy a house.	I'd like to buy a house.
❶ _____	She would like to have a cat.	_____
❷ They want to visit Tokyo.	_____	_____
❸ _____	_____	I'd like to eat an orange.
❹ _____	You would like to learn Spanish.	_____
❺ _____	_____	We'd like to go to a café.
❻ He wants to live in Germany.	_____	_____
❼ _____	We would like to swim in a lake.	_____

 47.2 RELIEZ CHAQUE IMAGE À LA DESCRIPTION CORRESPONDANTE.

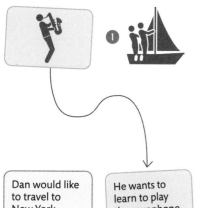

❶   ❷   ❸   ❹   ❺

| Dan would like to travel to New York. | He wants to learn to play the saxophone. | They'd like to go sailing on a sailboat. | We want to go on vacation to Tahiti. | Sharon wants to read her book. | Doug would like to climb a mountain. |

🔊

47.3 RÉCRIVEZ LES PHRASES SUIVANTES EN PLAÇANT LES MOTS ENTRE PARENTHÈSES AU BON ENDROIT.

She would like go to Paris. [to]
She would like to go to Paris.

① Douglas to have pasta. [wants]

② They'd to go home tomorrow. [like]

③ Does Chris want go swimming later? [to]

④ Sheila doesn't to see Paul. [want]

⑤ Would you to visit us tomorrow? [like]

⑥ Our children want go to college. [to]

⑦ She'd to buy a new cell phone. [like]

⑧ Jenny to go shopping on Friday. [wants]

⑨ Simon like to be a doctor. [would]

⑩ I like to have a hamburger. [would]

⑪ Would like to be a vet? [you]

⑫ Chloe want to eat that pizza. [doesn't]

⑬ You want to read this book? [Do]

⑭ They like to watch TV. [would]

⑮ She wants go to the party. [to]

 **47.4 UTILISEZ LE SCHÉMA POUR CRÉER 12 PHRASES, PUIS LISEZ-LES À VOIX HAUTE.**

I'd like to drive to Miami.

I'd like		
We want	to drive	to Miami.
Greg wants	to travel	around America.

47.5 ÉCOUTEZ L'ENREGISTREMENT, PUIS COCHEZ LA BONNE RÉPONSE.

Deux amis parlent
de ce qu'ils veulent faire.

Does Pete want to play basketball later?
Yes, he does. ☐ **No, he doesn't.** ☑

❹ Does Kat want to buy a new dress?
Yes, she does. ☐ **No, she doesn't.** ☐

❶ Would Pete like to read his book?
Yes, he would. ☐ **No, he wouldn't.** ☐

❺ Does Kat want to go to see a movie?
Yes, she does. ☐ **No, she doesn't.** ☐

❷ Does Pete want to stay at home tomorrow?
Yes, he does. ☐ **No, he doesn't.** ☐

❻ Does Pete want to go to a French restaurant?
Yes, he does. ☐ **No, he doesn't.** ☐

❸ Would Pete like to go shopping?
Yes, he would. ☐ **No, he wouldn't.** ☐

❼ Does Kat want to order spaghetti at the restaurant?
Yes, she does. ☐ **No, she doesn't.** ☐

47.6 ÉCRIVEZ LES MOTS SUIVANTS DANS LE BON ORDRE AFIN DE RECONSTITUER LES PHRASES.

| like | go | you | to | Would | to | year? | New York | next |

Would you like to go to New York next year?

❶ | Austria. | to | Marie | go | snowboarding | wants | in |

_____

❷ | doesn't | go | school | to | Mario | today. | want | to |

_____

❸ | climb | mountain. | wants | to | that | She |

_____

❹ | in | Tony | play | to | would | Scotland. | like | golf |

_____

◀))

47.7 RÉCRIVEZ LES PHRASES SUIVANTES EN CORRIGEANT LES ERREURS.

Would you want to go home?
Would you like to go home?

1 Do you want go home now?

2 Claude would likes to learn French.

3 He would likes to go swimming.

4 Paolo wants get a new cat.

5 Would you like visit China?

6 He's like to go to work later today.

7 Peter want to go to college next year.

8 They doesn't want to go to school today.

9 My sister want to go to Greece this summer.

🔊

47.8 RÉCRIVEZ LES PHRASES SUIVANTES À LA FORME INTERROGATIVE, PUIS LISEZ-LES À VOIX HAUTE.

She wants to play chess.

Does she want to play chess?

1 Peter would like to go fishing.

2 Marion wants to play tennis on Saturday.

3 He'd like to visit India.

4 Mr. Evans would like to play chess tonight.

5 We'd like to play squash this evening.

6 Sam wants to go to the park again.

7 They'd like to travel around China.

🔊

48 Parler de vos études

Lorsque vous évoquez vos études, vous pouvez utiliser « I would » et « I want » pour parler des sujets que vous voudriez apprendre. Utilisez les adverbes pour dire à quel point vous souhaitez les étudier.

⚙ Grammaire Les adverbes et les articles
Aa Vocabulaire Les matières scolaires
🧩 Compétence Parler de vos ambitions

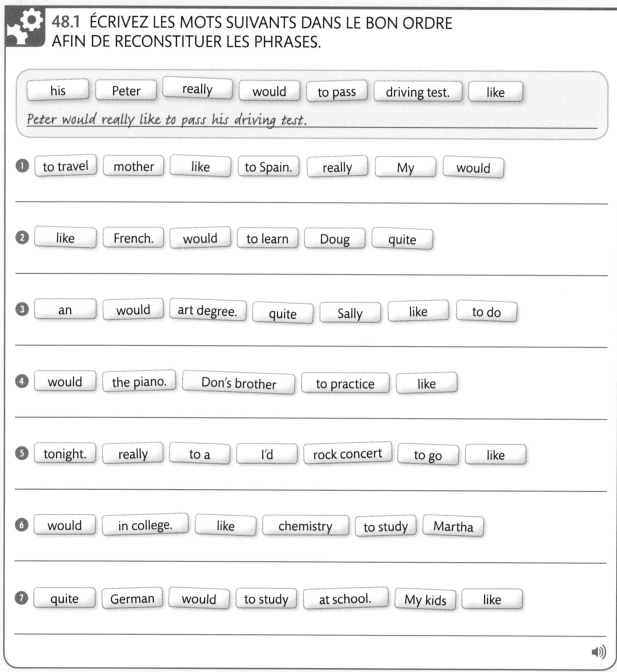

48.1 ÉCRIVEZ LES MOTS SUIVANTS DANS LE BON ORDRE AFIN DE RECONSTITUER LES PHRASES.

| his | Peter | really | would | to pass | driving test. | like |

Peter would really like to pass his driving test.

1 | to travel | mother | like | to Spain. | really | My | would |

2 | like | French. | would | to learn | Doug | quite |

3 | an | would | art degree. | quite | Sally | like | to do |

4 | would | the piano. | Don's brother | to practice | like |

5 | tonight. | really | to a | I'd | rock concert | to go | like |

6 | would | in college. | like | chemistry | to study | Martha |

7 | quite | German | would | to study | at school. | My kids | like |

48.2 RÉCRIVEZ LES PHRASES EN AJOUTANT LE MOT ENTRE PARENTHÈSES AU BON ENDROIT.

She'd like to do a French degree. [quite]

> *She'd quite like to do a French degree.*

1 Edith would like to read her new book. [really]

2 They'd like to go to a concert. [really]

3 I'd like to go to France on vacation. [really]

4 Jean-Paul would like to speak to you. [quite]

5 We'd like to eat pizza tonight. [quite]

6 Jeremy would like to play his piano. [really]

7 They'd like to pass their chemistry exam. [really]

8 Sophie would like to speak Mandarin. [quite]

9 David would like to visit his son. [really]

48.3 UTILISEZ LE SCHÉMA POUR CRÉER 14 PHRASES, PUIS LISEZ-LES À VOIX HAUTE.

> *I'd really like to improve my English.*

| I'd / Sam would / We'd | really / quite | like | to improve my English. / to learn Japanese. / to do a history degree. |

Aa 48.4 ENTOUREZ LES 8 MOTS DE LA LISTE DANS LA GRILLE.

```
M  G  D  P  R  D  R  A  M  A
U  A  V  R  E  H  K  Q  V (H
S  E  T  A  V  J  E  D  S  I
I  T  V  H  I  M  X  E  E  S
C  S  U  R  E  V  A  G  E  T
E  A  D  D  W  R  M  R  D  O
R  M  Z  C  Y  H  S  E  T  R
K  A  K  E  L  K  X  E  Y  Y)
F  N  A  R  H  M  S  U  A  N
```

review   music   study   drama

~~history~~   math   degree   exams

48.5 BARREZ LE MOT INCORRECT DANS CHAQUE PHRASE.

> Jim went to bed / ~~the bed~~ hours ago.

1. Phillipa goes to college / the college.

2. Rome is beautiful city / a beautiful city.

3. We are at home / the home at the moment.

4. Sharon goes to the school / school at 9am.

5. College / The college is far away.

6. Peter goes to bed / the bed at 10pm.

7. My uncle is at mosque / the mosque today.

8. Jim goes to church / the church on Sundays.

9. Sean leaves home / a home at 7:30am.

10. Seb lives next to hospital / the hospital.

🔊

48.6 COCHEZ LES PHRASES CORRECTES.

> Shirley works in the hospital in Bigton. ☑
> Shirley works in hospital in Bigton. ☐

1. Carol leaves work at 6pm every day. ☐
   Carol leaves a work at 6pm every day. ☐

2. Jane can drive you to school tomorrow. ☐
   Jane can drive you to a school tomorrow. ☐

3. Chris lives across from hospital. ☐
   Chris lives across from the hospital. ☐

4. Carl is at a home at the moment. ☐
   Carl is at home at the moment. ☐

5. Julia has beautiful horse. ☐
   Julia has a beautiful horse. ☐

6. The hospital isn't very far. ☐
   Hospital isn't very far. ☐

7. We go to bed at 11pm usually. ☐
   We go to the bed at 11pm usually. ☐

8. Ottersley is a beautiful town. ☐
   Ottersley is beautiful town. ☐

9. Your shoes are under bed. ☐
   Your shoes are under the bed. ☐

🔊

48.7 RÉCRIVEZ LES PHRASES SUIVANTES EN CORRIGEANT LES ERREURS.

> Does your sister work in school?
> *Does your sister work in a school?*

1 Sally is in the hospital. She is ill.

2 York is the pretty town.

3 She is at a home now.

4 Lizzie goes to the church on Sundays.

5 Bob is at the work at the moment.

6 Christopher has new car.

7 Jim goes to the bed early on Sundays.

8 Carlos is the very talented boy.

9 Sarah and John are great team.

10 Mary bought the three new pens.

11 He jumped into a water and started swimming.

12 New York is the beautiful city.

13 A children were playing in the sun.

14 I can't play the soccer on Monday.

15 Can you play a classical guitar?

🔊

48.8 ÉCOUTEZ L'ENREGISTREMENT, PUIS RELIEZ CHAQUE IMAGE AU PRÉNOM CORRESPONDANT.

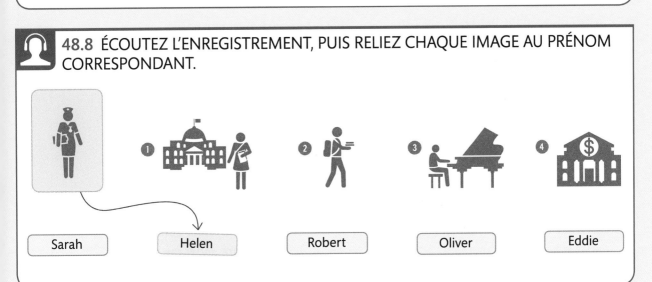

Réponses

1.1 🔊
1. I'm Natalie.
2. My name's Sue.
3. I'm Ryan.
4. My name's Mia.
5. My name's Amelia.

1.2
A 3 B 1 C 2 D 6 E 4 F 5

1.3 🔊
1. Hi! I am Charlotte.
2. Hi! My name is Charlotte.
3. Hello! I am Charlotte.
4. Hello! My name is Charlotte.
5. Hi! I am Carla.
6. Hi! My name is Carla.
7. Hello! I am Carla.
8. Hello! My name is Carla.
9. Hi! I am Fatima.
10. Hi! My name is Fatima.
11. Hello! I am Fatima.
12. Hello! My name is Fatima.

1.4
1. N-o-a-h A-n-d-e-r-s-o-n
2. M-a-s-o-n H-u-g-h-e-s
3. E-l-i S-a-n-d-e-r-s
4. A-l-i-c-i-a
5. Z-o-e S-p-i-e-g-e-l-m-a-n
6. B-e-n
7. N-o-r-a J-a-m-e-s
8. A-m-i-r A-n-s-a-r-i
9. N-i-n-a E-d-w-a-r-d-s
10. L-u-c-y
11. A-m-a-n S-h-a-r-m-a
12. A-i-d-e-n
13. K-e-i-t-h
14. F-i-o-n-a
15. J-a-m-e-s T-h-o-m-a-s

1.5 🔊
1. My name is Terry, T-e-r-r-y.
2. My last name is Singh, S-i-n-g-h.

3. I'm Mario, M-a-r-i-o.
4. My name is Yasmin Khan, Y-a-s-m-i-n K-h-a-n.
5. I am Jacob, J-a-c-o-b.

2.1 🔊
1. South Korea
2. Thailand
3. Greece
4. Poland
5. Argentina
6. Russia
7. Australia
8. Canada
9. Philippines
10. Pakistan
11. Slovakia
12. Republic of Ireland
13. China
14. Portugal
15. South Africa
16. Brazil
17. Netherlands
18. Spain
19. Czech Republic
20. Singapore
21. Egypt
22. Mongolia
23. United Kingdom
24. France
25. Mexico
26. India
27. United States of America
28. Japan
29. Indonesia
30. United Arab Emirates
31. New Zealand
32. Germany
33. Austria
34. Switzerland

3.1 🔊
1. 85 2. 21 3. 90 4. 17 5. 84 6. 62
7. 47 8. 50 9. 71 10. 12 11. 33

3.2 🔊
1. Chloe is thirty-one years old.
2. Heidi is fifty-two years old.
3. Zach is sixteen years old.
4. Charlie is ten years old.
5. Marcel is eighty years old.
6. Claire is twenty-one years old.
7. Dan is thirty-six years old.
8. Eleanor is twenty-eight years old.
9. Rebecca is forty-three years old.

3.3 🔊
1. I am twenty-three years old.
2. I am thirty-two years old.
3. I am sixty-eight years old.
4. Dan is twenty-three years old.
5. Dan is thirty-two years old.
6. Dan is sixty-eight years old.
7. You are twenty-three years old.
8. You are thirty-two years old.
9. You are sixty-eight years old.

3.4 🔊
1. Abe **is** 72 years old. She **is** Japanese.
2. Mia and Leo **are** 12. They **are** from Italy.
3. Chantal **is** 66 years old. She **is** French.
4. Amir and Aamna **are** 90 years old. They **are** from Pakistan.
5. I **am** 24 years old. I **am** Irish.
6. Max **is** 47 years old. He **is** German.
7. We **are** 38 years old. We **are** from New Zealand.
8. My sister **is** 4 years old. She **is** from Canada.

4.1 🔊
1. grandfather
2. father
3. uncle
4. sister
5. son
6. daughter
7. grandson
8. granddaughter

4.2 🔊
1. cat
2. chicken

3 rabbit
4 tortoise
5 parrot
6 dog
7 fish
8 snake
9 pig
10 horse
11 guinea pig

05

5.1 ◄))
1 **Their** dog is called Beth.
2 **His** tortoise is 50 years old.
3 **My** cat is called Sam.
4 **Our** lion is from Kenya.
5 **Your** rabbit eats grass.
6 Here is **its** bed.
7 **Their** snake is called Sid.
8 Buster is **my** monkey.
9 **Your** parrot is from Venezuela.
10 **Her** cat is called Tabatha.
11 **Their** monkey is from Morocco.
12 **Her** pig lives on a farm.
13 **His** horse is called Prancer.
14 **Our** chicken lives in the garden.

5.2 ◄))
1 Fido is **my** dog.
2 Cookie is **his** cat.
3 It is **our** chicken.
4 Ziggy is **your** parrot.
5 Hiss is **their** snake.
6 Max is **our** monkey.
7 It is **her** rabbit.
8 Ed is **my** horse.
9 Rex is **your** dog.
10 Nemo is **her** fish.
11 It is **our** sheep.

5.3 ◄))
1 **This** is her rabbit.
2 **This** is its ball.
3 **That** is our dog.
4 **This** is his snake.
5 **That** is my horse.

5.4 ◄))
1 Their fish is called Bob.
2 This is their cow.

3 His snake is called Harold.
4 Her cat is 12 years old.
5 Barney is our rabbit.

5.5 ◄))
1. This is her cat.
2. This is her parrot.
3. This is their cat.
4. This is their parrot.
5. This is my cat.
6. This is my parrot.
7. That is her cat.
8. That is her parrot.
9. That is their cat.
10. That is their parrot.
11. That is my cat.
12. That is my parrot.

06

6.1 ◄))
1 Joe and Greg's dog
2 Dolly's granddaughters
3 Sue's house
4 Pete and Aziz's snake

6.2
1 Arthur is **Sam's grandfather.**
2 Frank is **Sam's father.**
3 Charlotte is **Sam's mother.**
4 Micky is **Sam's brother.**
5 Sally is **Sam's sister.**
6 Ronaldo is **Sam's friend.**
7 Rebecca is **Sam's cousin.**

6.3
1 True 2 False 3 False
4 True 5 False

6.4 ◄))
1 That's my grandparents' car.
2 These are Pete and Omar's cats.
3 I am Sally's granddaughter.
4 Where is your parents' house?
5 Samantha is Barry's new wife.

6.5 ◄))
1 Sooty is **my brothers'** cat.
2 They are **Tammy's** parents.
3 This is our **children's** snake.
4 My **parents'** house is small.

07

7.1 ◄))
1 notebook
2 sunglasses
3 keys
4 pen
5 necklace
6 newspaper
7 ID card
8 letter
9 toothbrush
10 hairbrush
11 bottle of water
12 laptop
13 earphones
14 pencil
15 dictionary
16 apple
17 book
18 tablet
19 mirror
20 coins
21 passport
22 magazine
23 camera
24 glasses
25 map
26 umbrella
27 sandwich

08

8.1 ◄))
1 **These** are my mom's glasses.
2 **Those** are Samantha's keys.
3 **This** is Tom's umbrella.
4 **This** is my dog.
5 **Those** are Pete's books.
6 **That** is your newspaper.
7 **These** are my tickets.
8 **These** are Marge's earrings.
9 **These** are his daughters.
10 **That** is my teacher.
11 **That** is your watch.

8.2
1 This is my letter.
2 These are my purses.

3 That is Greg's key.
4 Those are my cats.
5 This is my sister's pencil.
6 Those are your dictionaries.
7 These are Dan's houses.
8 That is Stan's book.
9 That is my brother.

8.3 🔊
1 pencils
2 fishes / fish
3 brothers
4 diaries
5 necklaces
6 brushes
7 watches
8 boxes
9 dictionaries
10 sisters
11 umbrellas
12 laptops

8.4 🔊
1 brushes
2 boxes
3 dictionaries
4 dogs
5 notebooks
6 toothbrushes
7 books
8 pencils
9 letters
10 newspapers
11 glasses
12 passports
13 magazines

8.5
1 three sandwiches
2 two necklaces
3 four bags
4 three toothbrushes
5 two diaries / planners
6 two cats
7 one apple

8.6 🔊
1 his
2 its
3 hers
4 yours
5 theirs
6 ours

8.7 🔊
1 This dog is his.
2 Those books are mine.
3 That fish is yours.
4 These bags are theirs.
5 These boxes are ours.

8.8
1 That dog is yours.
2 These sandwiches are Dan's.
3 That bag is hers.
4 Those sandwiches are ours.
5 That purse is Stacey's.
6 This key is his.
7 This newspaper is theirs.
8 That necklace is Linda's.
9 Those children are ours.

8.9 🔊
1 **These** are my books.
2 **This** is your dog.
3 **These** are her bags.
4 **These** are their boxes.
5 **This** is my toothbrush.
6 **This** is his diary.
7 **This** is your apple.
8 **These** are my apples.
9 **These** are your glasses.
10 **These** are Kevin's keys.
11 **This** is my dad's car.

8.10
DÉTERMINANTS : **your**, **his**, **my**
PRONOMS : **hers**, **mine**

09

9.1 🔊
1 pilot
2 fire fighter
3 gardener
4 driver
5 electrician
6 actor
7 nurse
8 farmer
9 chef
10 receptionist
11 businesswoman
12 police officer
13 dentist

14 vet
15 teacher
16 businessman
17 mechanic
18 waiter
19 engineer
20 cleaner
21 artist
22 hairdresser
23 waitress
24 construction worker
25 doctor
26 sales assistant
27 judge

10

10.1
1 He / She is a doctor.
2 You are teachers.
3 I am a hairdresser.
4 We are mechanics.
5 You are a cleaner.
6 They are chefs.
7 He / She is an actor.
8 They are vets.
9 I am a police officer.
10 You are farmers.
11 You are a waitress.
12 We are gardeners.
13 I am an artist.

10.2 🔊
1 I **am an** actor.
2 He **is a** teacher.
3 He **is a** chef.
4 You **are an** engineer.
5 We **are** hairdressers.
6 They **are** farmers.
7 You **are a** vet.
8 I **am a** waiter.
9 She **is a** nurse.

10.3 🔊
1 I **am** a vet.
2 She **is** a businesswoman.
3 We **are** doctors.
4 They **are** teachers.
5 He **is** a mechanic.
6 I **am** a driver.
7 We **are** receptionists.

8 They **are** waitresses.
9 She **is** a police officer.
10 I **am** a judge.
11 You **are** a nurse.
12 We **are** farmers.
13 She **is** a sales assistant.
14 I **am** a chef.

1 laboratory
2 restaurant
3 garden
4 hospital
5 school

1 He works **in** a doctor's office.
2 We work **on** a farm.
3 My dad works **on** a building site.
4 My sister works **in** a café.
5 We work **in** people's gardens.
6 Dan works **in** a hospital.
7 I work **in** a restaurant.
8 We work **in** a school.
9 Chris works **in** a supermarket.

1 Abby **is a nurse**. She **works in a hospital**.
2 Julie **is an engineer**. She **works on a construction site**.
3 Simon **is a gardener**. He **works in a park**.
4 Adam **is a police officer**. He **works in a police station**.
5 Max **is a farmer**. He **works on a farm**.
6 Carol **is a hairdresser**. She **works in a beauty salon**.

1 Sam is a **doctor** and she works with **patients**.
2 Gabriella is a **chef** and she works with **food**.
3 Dan is a **vet** and he works with **animals**.
4 John is a **farmer** and he works with **crops**.
5 Tom is an **actor** and he works in a **theater**.

1 gardener
2 teacher
3 doctor
4 waiter

5 hairdressers
6 actor
7 contractor

11

1 It's four thirty.
2 It's seven fifty.
3 It's midnight.
4 It's a quarter after six.
5 It's half past eight.
6 It's three thirty.
7 It's a quarter to nine.
8 It's five forty-five.

1 08:15
2 08:30
3 11:15
4 09:20
5 11:00
6 07:15
7 03:25
8 09:45
9 06:28
10 05:30
11 10:00
12 02:30
13 08:15

1 11:15
2 11:00
3 8:24
4 3:30
5 2:45
6 5:25
7 3:49
8 2:15
9 9:00
10 7:45
11 11:30
12 9:25
13 10:15
14 11:20
15 1:55
16 6:45
17 6:45

1 It's a quarter to ten. / It's nine forty-five.
2 It's four o'clock.
3 It's ten twenty.
4 It's half past eleven. / It's eleven thirty.
5 It's three forty-seven.
6 It's a quarter past three. / It's three fifteen.
7 It's half past six. / It's six thirty.
8 It's eight twenty-two.
9 It's one twenty-five.

12

1 buy groceries
2 take a bath
3 have lunch
4 clear the table
5 start work
6 wash your face
7 get up
8 cook dinner
9 brush your hair
10 leave work
11 finish work
12 brush your teeth
13 go home
14 have dinner
15 go to school
16 get dressed
17 go to bed
18 take a shower
19 wake up
20 iron a shirt
21 dawn
22 day
23 dusk
24 night
25 do the dishes
26 have breakfast
27 walk the dog

13

1 Marion has a shower at 6:45am.
2 Marion has breakfast at 7am.
3 Marion brushes her teeth at 7:20am.

4 Marion goes to work at 7:30am.

5 Marion gets the bus at 7:45am.

6 Marion gets to work at 8:30am.

7 Marion leaves work at 5pm.

13.2 🔊

1 I **wake** up at 6:30am.

2 He **gets** up at 6am.

3 She **has** a shower at 7am.

4 They **have** cereal for breakfast.

5 He **has** a shower before breakfast.

6 She **leaves** home at 7:15am.

7 The bus **goes** every half hour.

8 I **get** to work at 8:30am.

9 He **starts** work at 9am.

10 She **takes** an hour for lunch.

11 I **go** to the sandwich shop for lunch.

12 They **eat** lunch in the canteen.

13 He **finishes** work at 5pm.

14 They **go** home on the bus.

15 He **washes** his car every weekend.

16 I **watch** TV after dinner.

17 They **go** to bed at 11pm.

18 He **sleeps** for eight hours.

13.3 🔊

1 He **has**

2 It **starts**

3 He **leaves**

4 She **gets up**

5 It **goes**

6 She **wakes up**

7 He **washes**

8 She **watches**

9 It **finishes**

13.4 🔊

1 He **gets** up at 6:30am.

2 He **has** breakfast at 7am.

3 She **leaves** home at 8am.

4 I **drive** to work.

5 I **have** lunch in the park.

6 I **work** eight hours every day.

7 He **goes** to bed at 10:30pm.

13.5 🔊

1 goes

2 washes

3 wakes

4 gets

5 watches

6 leaves

7 has

8 finishes

14

14.1 🔊

1 I go to the movies **on** the weekend.

2 Joe starts work at 6pm **on** Mondays.

3 You watch TV **in** the afternoon.

4 Harry plays tennis **on** Wednesdays.

5 Lin goes swimming **in** the evening.

6 Alex goes fishing **on** the weekend.

7 He eats lunch at 1pm **on** Fridays.

8 Sam goes to the gym **in** the morning.

14.2 🔊

1 I work from Monday to Thursday.

2 My sister goes swimming every day.

3 We go to the gym on Saturdays.

4 You read the newspaper on Sundays.

5 Peter goes to work on the weekend.

6 Jennifer goes to a café on Fridays.

7 Sam and Pete work from 9am to 5pm.

14.3 🔊

1 Pam works **from** Monday **to** Friday.

2 I work at home **on** Thursdays.

3 Tom goes to the cinema **on** Fridays.

4 I play soccer **on / at** the weekend.

5 They work **from** Monday **to** Thursday.

6 We go to bed at 9pm **on** Mondays.

7 Laura goes shopping **on** Tuesdays.

8 Peter gets up at 8am **on** Mondays.

9 We go the gym **on** Thursdays.

10 Gerald reads a book **on / at** the weekend.

11 Jane swims **from** Monday **to** Friday.

12 John takes a bath **on** Fridays.

13 Lizzy starts work at 9am **on** Fridays.

14.4 🔊

1 Dan goes to the gym three times a week.

2 Sam goes to the cinema twice a week.

3 We go to bed at 11:30pm every day.

4 Joe goes to college five times a week.

5 Clarice washes her clothes once a week.

6 Jennifer gets up at 10am twice a week.

7 We eat dinner at 7pm every day.

14.5 🔊

1 Bob **goes swimming** on Thursdays.

2 I play tennis **on the weekend / at the weekend**.

3 Jane and Tom go to the gym **three times** a week.

4 Angus works from **Monday to Thursday**.

5 I go to the movies **on the weekend / at the weekend**.

6 Sam goes to **college on Wednesdays**.

7 Jenny gets up **at 7am** every day.

8 Peter **works from** Monday to Friday.

9 Nina **goes to bed** at 11pm every day.

14.6

1 False 2 True 3 False 4 True

5 False 6 True

14.7

A 3

B 6

C 4

D 5

E 1

F 2

14.8

1 farmer

2 nurse

3 restaurant

4 8am

5 Saturday

6 theater

7 three days

8 waitress

9 6pm

15

15.1 🔊

1 Paula is not a teacher.

2 We are not from England.

3 This is not my phone.

4 Kirsty is not 18 years old.

5 Frank is not my father.

6 This is not my purse.

7 They are not engineers.

8 That is not a salon.

9 Kim is not a teacher.

15.2 🔊

1 That **is not** a castle.

2 They **are not** at school.

3 He **is not** a grandfather.

4 We **are not** engineers.

5 She **is not** 70 years old.

6 You **are not** French.

7 This **is not** my dog.

8 I **am not** a doctor.

9 It **is not** 11 o'clock.

15.3

A 3

B 1

C 2

D 4

15.4

1 Fredo is not a chef.
Fredo isn't a chef.

2 Susie's not my cat.
Susie isn't my cat.

3 My dad is not at work.
My dad's not at work.

4 They are not at the theater.
They aren't at the theater.

15.5

1 True

2 False

3 True

4 True

5 False

15.6 ◀ঠ

1 This **isn't** his umbrella.

2 Pedro **isn't** Spanish.

3 Pete and Terry **aren't** hairdressers.

4 It **isn't** a snake.

5 My cousins **aren't** 21 years old.

6 It **isn't** half past six.

7 **I'm not** your friend.

15.7

1 True

2 True

3 False

4 True

5 True

6 False

15.8 ◀ঠ

1 I'm a student. I'm not a teacher.

2 I'm 30 years old. I'm not 40.

3 I'm a farmer. I'm not a police officer.

4 I'm French. I'm not English.

5 I'm an uncle. I'm not a father.

6 I'm 18. I'm not 21.

7 I'm a waitress. I'm not a chef.

8 I'm Spanish. I'm not Italian.

15.9 ◀ঠ

1 You're 28. You're not 29.

2 You're a scientist. You're not a gardener.

3 You're Austrian. You're not English.

4 You're a contractor. You're not an actor.

5 You're 16. You're not 18.

6 You're an uncle. You're not a grandfather.

7 You're a mechanic. You're not an engineer.

8 You're a police officer. You're not a firefighter.

15.10 ◀ঠ

1. I'm not at work.

2. I'm not an actor.

3. I'm not American.

4. I'm not 40 years old.

5. You aren't at work.

6. You aren't an actor.

7. You aren't American.

8. You aren't 40 years old.

9. She isn't at work.

10. She isn't an actor.

11. She isn't American.

12. She isn't 40 years old.

16

16.1 ◀ঠ

1 Jane **does not** walk to work.

2 My brother **does not** watch TV.

3 I **do not** read a book in the evening.

4 Frank **does not** work at the museum.

5 They **do not** go dancing on the weekend.

6 We **do not** go to work on Fridays.

7 I **do not** get up at 7:30am.

8 You **do not** have a car.

9 My dad **does not** work in an office.

10 You **do not** have a dog.

11 My sister **does not** work with children.

12 They **do not** live in the country.

13 Freddie **does not** eat meat.

16.2 ◀ঠ

1 Tony doesn't live in New York.

2 Sebastian doesn't work on a farm.

3 My uncle doesn't work in a factory.

4 We don't play soccer on Thursdays.

5 I don't learn German at school.

6 Carlo doesn't work on Mondays.

7 You don't take a bath at night.

16.3

1 Tim does not play tennis.
Tim doesn't play tennis.

2 You do not have a black cat.
You don't have a black cat.

3 Jules does not read a book every day.
Jules doesn't read a book every day.

4 Sam does not work in a restaurant.
Sam doesn't work in a restaurant.

5 They do not play soccer.
They don't play soccer.

6 Emily does not work with animals.
Emily doesn't work with animals.

7 Mel and Greg do not have a car.
Mel and Greg don't have a car.

8 You do not work in a factory.
You don't work in a factory.

16.4 ◀ঠ

1 Chloe **doesn't** play tennis with her friends.

2 You **don't** work outside.

3 Sal and Doug **don't** have a car.

4 We **don't** watch TV at home.

5 Mrs. O'Brien **doesn't** work in an office.

6 You **don't** wake up at 6am.

7 They **don't** eat lunch at 1pm.

8 Virginia **doesn't** speak good English.

9 Trevor **doesn't** live near here.

10 My dad **doesn't** live in Los Angeles.

11 David **doesn't** play chess.

16.5 ◀ঠ

1 Jean doesn't cycle to work.

2 They don't live in the city.

3 Mr. James doesn't go to the theater.

4 He doesn't read a newspaper.

5 My cousins don't have tickets.

6 Sally doesn't go to the gym.

7 Our dog doesn't have a ball.

8 I don't have a laptop.

9 My mom doesn't get up at 7:30am.

10 You don't live in the country.

11 Claude doesn't have a dictionary.

16.6

1 False **2** False **3** True **4** False
5 True **6** False **7** True

16.7

1 Carla **2** Sam **3** Greg **4** Carla
5 Sam **6** Greg **7** Sam **8** Carla

16.8 🔊

1. I don't go swimming.
2. I don't have a car.
3. I don't speak Japanese.
4. Frank doesn't go swimming.
5. Frank doesn't have a car.
6. Frank doesn't speak Japanese.
7. We don't go swimming.
8. We don't have a car.
9. We don't speak Japanese.

17

17.1 🔊

1. Is this his passport?
2. Is it 6 o'clock?
3. Are Doug and Jim hairdressers?
4. Are these my glasses?
5. Is Sally his sister?
6. Are those your letters?
7. Is she a nurse?
8. Is this your snake?
9. Is it 3pm?
10. Is his wife a chef?
11. Are Katie and Jess my friends?

17.2 🔊

1. Are you an actor?
2. Are you a teacher?
3. Are you engineers?
4. Are they engineers?
5. Is she a teacher?
6. Is she an actor?

17.3 🔊

1. **Is** Dorota at school?
2. **Is** this your parrot?
3. **Is** there a bank near here?
4. **Are** you a gardener?
5. **Are** these Jean's keys?
6. **Is** there a castle in your town?
7. **Is** that your bag?
8. **Are** they your cousins?
9. **Are** they from France?
10. **Is** she Sam's sister?
11. **Is** this my burger?
12. **Is** there a church in this town?
13. **Are** those Brooke's shirts?

17.4 🔊

1. Is Paula from Italy?
2. Is it half past two?
3. Is Ronaldo your father?
4. Is there a bank on your street?
5. Are these your dad's glasses?
6. Is this your laptop?
7. Are those Katherine's books?

17.5 🔊

1. **Do** you work in a hospital?
2. **Does** your dog like children?
3. **Do** you get up at 10am on Sundays?
4. **Does** Simone work with children?
5. **Do** they live in the town?
6. **Do** we finish work at 3pm today?
7. **Does** Frank play tennis with Pete?

17.6 🔊

1. **Do** you read a newspaper every day?
2. **Does** he go to bed at 11pm?
3. **Do** they live in a castle?
4. **Does** Pedro come from Bolivia?
5. **Does** she work with children?
6. **Do** Claire and Sam eat lunch at 2pm?
7. **Does** your brother work with animals?
8. **Does** Tim play soccer on Mondays?
9. **Do** they work in a café?
10. **Do** you have a shower in the evening?
11. **Do** we start work at 10am on Thursdays?
12. **Does** Pamela work in a bank?

17.7 🔊

1. Do they work in a museum?
2. Do you work with children?
3. Does Shane live in Sydney?
4. Does John play tennis on Wednesdays?
5. Do Yves and Marie eat dinner at 6pm?
6. Does Seth work in a post office?

17.8

1. No 2. No 3. Yes 4. Yes
5. Yes 6. No 7. Yes

17.9 🔊

1. **Do** you go to a restaurant on Fridays?
2. **Does** Peter live near the museum?
3. **Do** Sam and Doug work with animals?
4. **Does** she get up at 7am on the weekend?
5. **Do** they play tennis in the evening?

18

18.1 🔊

1. Yes, I do.
2. No, they aren't.
3. Yes, it is.
4. Yes, she does.
5. Yes, it is.

18.2 🔊

1. No, **I don't.**
2. Yes, **she is.**
3. No, **he doesn't.**
4. No, **they don't.**
5. Yes, **he is.**

18.3

1. No, she isn't.
2. No, she doesn't.
3. No, it isn't.
4. Yes, she does.
5. No, she doesn't.

18.4

1. True 2. False 3. False 4. True
5. True 6. Not given 7. True

19

19.1 🔊

1. Franco. And yours?
2. I'm fine, thanks.
3. It's half past seven.
4. That's my wife, Vicky.
5. It's across from the bank.
6. It's his birthday.
7. He's the boy with red hair.
8. It's at 3 o'clock.
9. It's on Saturday.
10. I'm twenty-three.

19.2 🔊

1. **Why** does the dog keep barking?
2. **Where** are your parents now?
3. **Who** is your brother?
4. **What** is your name?
5. **When** is Carla's birthday?
6. **Where** is your sister's house?
7. **Which** car is yours?

8 **When** are your exams?
9 **Where** did you park the car?
10 **Why** are you sad?
11 **When** can I go home?
12 **Where** does your brother live?
13 **What** is your first memory?

19.3
1 84 years old
2 Near the supermarket
3 At a school
4 She's a receptionist
5 19

19.4 ◀))
1 Which shirt do you prefer?
2 Where does your son go to college?
3 How do you get to work?
4 Where do you go swimming?
5 What time do you go to bed?
6 When does Jane start work?
7 What do you eat for breakfast?

19.5 ◀))
1 **What** do you study?
2 **Which** do you want?
3 **Which** building is your college?
4 **Where** do you live?
5 **What** time do you wake up?
6 **How** many shirts do you own?
7 **What** do you want for lunch?
8 **When** does the course finish?
9 **What** do you do in the evening?

19.6 ◀))
1 Which school does he go to?
2 Why does Kevin work there?
3 Where does your friend live?
4 Where is your car?
5 What does your brother do?

19.7 ◀))
1 How is your uncle?
2 Which woman is your wife?
3 Where do you work?
4 What time is the meeting?
5 When do you finish work tonight?

19.8 ◀))
1. Where does he play soccer?
2. Where does Jane play soccer?
3. Where do you play soccer?
4. Where does he live?

5. Where does Jane live?
6. Where do you live?
7. When does he play soccer?
8. When does he finish work?
9. When do you play soccer?
10. When do you finish work?
11. When does Jane play soccer?
12. When does Jane finish work?

19.9
1 Blois
2 Janet
3 Near the castle
4 French bread
5 In a café
6 Explore the old town
7 About 1,000 years old
8 Some beautiful paintings

20

20.1 ◀))
1 school
2 police station
3 supermarket
4 bridge
5 hotel
6 here
7 post office
8 mosque
9 town
10 park
11 library
12 airport
13 there
14 hospital
15 pharmacy
16 bank
17 train station
18 factory
19 bar
20 near
21 castle
22 bus station
23 restaurant
24 office building
25 swimming pool
26 café
27 far

21

21.1 ◀))
1 **There is** a station.
2 **There is** a swimming pool.
3 **There are** two theaters.
4 **There is** a factory.
5 **There are** two parks.
6 **There are** three cafés.

21.2 ◀))
1 There **isn't** a restaurant.
2 There **aren't** any schools.
3 There **isn't** a post office.
4 There **aren't** any cafés.
5 There **aren't** any bars.
6 There **isn't** a train station.
7 There **isn't** a library.
8 There **aren't** any supermarkets.
9 There **aren't** any parks.
10 There **isn't** a town hall.

21.3 ◀))
1. There is a hotel.
2. There is no hotel.
3. There are three parks.
4. There are no parks.
5. There aren't any parks.
6. There are three books.
7. There are no books.
8. There aren't any books.

21.4
A 3
B 2
C 1
D 4
E 5

21.5 ◀))
1 There isn't a school.
2 There aren't two churches.
3 There isn't a café.
4 There isn't a library.
5 There aren't two airports.
6 There aren't three hotels.
7 There aren't two parks.
8 There isn't a town hall.

21.6
1 churches
2 primary school

3 café
4 hospital
5 police officer

21.7 🔊
1 There is a supermarket.
2 There aren't any restaurants.
3 There are no hotels.
4 There are three schools.
5 There is a bus station.

21.8
1 False
2 True
3 False
4 False
5 True
6 False
7 True

21.9 🔊
1 There are three stores.
2 There are two castles.
3 There isn't a church.
4 There is a hospital.
5 There isn't a post office.

22

22.1 🔊
1 **The** new doctor is called Hilary.
2 Sammy is **a** nurse.
3 There is **a** bank downtown.
4 Is there **a** hospital near here?
5 **The** gym is near Sam's house.
6 There is **a** new café in town.
7 **The** hotel on Elm Lane is nice.
8 **The** new teacher is good.
9 There's **an** old theater in town.

22.2 🔊
1 I have **a** sister and **a** brother.
2 There is **a** library on Queens Road.
3 I bought **an** apple and **an** orange.
4 Is there **a** bank near here?
5 There is **a** café at the bus station.
6 My dad is **an** engineer.
7 There is **a** cell phone on the table.

22.3
Dear Bob and Sally,
We are in Glenmuir, **a** quiet town in Scotland. There's **a** castle and **a** cathedral here. They're beautiful, and **the** castle is really old. There are **some** interesting stores, which we visit every day. We also have **a** new friend here. He's called Alfonso and he works as **a** waiter in **the** Italian restaurant next to **the** shopping mall. He's great!
Jane

22.4 🔊
1 Are there **any** factories in your town?
2 Is there **a** gym downtown?
3 Are there **any** pencils in your bag?
4 Is there **an** old church on Station Road?
5 Is there **a** hospital in the town?
6 Is there **a** salon near here?
7 Is there **an** apple in the basket?
8 Are there **any** restaurants in your town?
9 Is there **a** library downtown?
10 Are there **any** books on the table?
11 Is there **a** café nearby?
12 Is there **a** cathedral in that town?
13 Is there **a** bank near the supermarket?
14 Are there **any** kittens here?
15 Is there **a** school in this neighborhood?

22.5 🔊
1 Is there a supermarket near here?
2 There are some cafés on Beech Road.
3 There are some horses on Frank's farm.
4 There are some hotels near the airport.

22.6 🔊
1 Is **there a** museum?
2 Are **there any** cafés?
3 Are **there any** parks near here?
4 Is **there a** mosque in the town?
5 Is **there an** airport in Saltforth?
6 Are **there any** factories in Halford?
7 Is **there a** castle in your town?

22.7 🔊
1 Yes, **there are.**
2 No, **there isn't.**
3 Yes, **there are.**
4 No, **there isn't.**
5 Yes, **there is.**
6 No, **there aren't.**
7 Yes, **there are.**

22.8
1 Stonehill
2 Museum
3 Lots
4 French
5 None
6 Two
7 Some

23

23.1 🔊
1 put
2 read
3 work
4 start
5 eat
6 have
7 stop
8 wake up
9 run
10 come
11 be

23.2 🔊
1 present simple
2 imperative
3 present simple
4 imperative
5 imperative
6 imperative
7 present simple
8 present simple
9 imperative

23.3 🔊
1 Go straight ahead. The swimming pool is opposite the station.
2 Take the second left. The school is opposite the factory.
3 Turn right and take the first left. The church is opposite the hotel.
4 Take the third left and go straight ahead. The theater is on the right.

23.4 🔊
1 Go past the house.
2 Take the second right.
3 Go straight ahead.
4 Turn left.
5 Take the third right.

23.5 🔊
1. on the left
2. opposite
3. on the right
4. behind
5. on the corner

23.6 🔊
1. Don't go straight ahead.
2. Don't come with me.
3. Don't take the first left.
4. Don't turn left at the intersection.
5. Don't read this daily planner.

23.7
A 5 B 2 C 6 D 4 E 9
F 8 G 3 H 7

23.8 🔊
1. The museum is **next to** the library.
2. The restaurant is **opposite** the store.
3. The hospital is **in front of** the theater.
4. The post office is **behind** the school.

24

24.1 🔊
1. My cousin lives and **works in Los Angeles.**
2. I play soccer and **basketball in the evening.**
3. There's a library and **a bookstore in my town.**
4. I eat two eggs and **a banana for breakfast.**
5. Pete's uncle and **aunt live in Arizona.**
6. I read a book and **watch TV on the weekend.**

24.2
1. restaurant
2. hospital
3. supermarket
4. movie theater
5. church

24.3 🔊
1. Three chefs and four waiters work in my hotel.
2. There's a park, a café, and a theater in Pella.
3. I have one aunt, two sisters, and a niece.
4. Ben eats breakfast, lunch, and dinner.
5. I play tennis and soccer.
6. We have a dog and a cat.
7. I read a book and take a bath on Sundays.
8. Jen speaks French, Spanish, and Japanese.
9. Pete has two dogs and a cat.

24.4 🔊
1. This is my brother and these are my sisters.
2. I speak English, but I don't speak French.
3. I play video games and I watch TV.
4. I have one uncle, but I don't have any aunts.
5. There are two stores and three hotels.
6. I eat lunch every day, but I don't eat breakfast.
7. There's a hotel, but there isn't a store.
8. I have a sandwich and an apple.
9. This is my house, but these aren't my keys.
10. Those are Sarah's magazines and that is her ID card.
11. This phone is Joe's, but this laptop isn't.

24.5 🔊
1. There's a library, a store, **and** a café.
2. There's a castle and a church **but** there isn't a museum.
3. Pete eats apples **but** doesn't eat bananas.
4. Greg reads magazines **and** a newspaper.
5. I have a calendar **and** a notebook.
6. He goes swimming **but** he doesn't play soccer.

24.6 🔊
1. Meg likes this restaurant **but** she doesn't like that café.
2. There are two schools **but** there isn't a library in my town.
3. I have a pen, a notebook, **and** a calendar in my bag.
4. My sister goes to the gym on Mondays **and** Thursdays.
5. Pedro works in a school **but** he isn't a teacher.

25

25.1 🔊
1. I am a busy man.
2. There is a new restaurant.
3. My friend is a beautiful woman.
4. We have a very old cat.
5. These are my new clothes.

25.2
1. good
2. beautiful
3. wonderful
4. busy
5. interesting
6. old
7. large

25.3 🔊
1. The children are small.
   They are small.
2. The waiter is good.
   He is good.
3. The dog is big.
   It is big.
4. The town is quiet.
   It is quiet.

25.4 🔊
1. new
2. large
3. bad
4. beautiful
5. old
6. slow
7. easy

25.5
1. False 2. True 3. False 4. True
5. False 6. True

25.6 🔊
1. **The** sea **is** blue **and the** sun **is** hot.
2. **The** beach **is** busy **and the** hotels **are** ugly.
3. **The** city **is** old **and the** buildings **are** beautiful.
4. **The** restaurant **is** good **and the** waiter **is** friendly.
5. **The** countryside **is** beautiful **and the** mountains **are** large.

⑥ **The** town **is** small **and the** shops **are** quiet.

25.7 ◀))
① **There are some** shops.
② **There are some** trees.
③ **There are lots of** cars.
④ **There are a few** churches.
⑤ **There are a few** flowers.
⑥ **There are some** cafés.
⑦ **There are a few** parks.

26

26.1 ◀))
① Fred works outside because **he's a farmer.**
② Mick travels to Switzerland because **he goes skiing there.**
③ Saul goes to bed late because **he works in a restaurant.**
④ I get up at 5am because **I'm a mailman.**
⑤ Marion goes to the library because **she's a student.**
⑥ Colin works with children because **he's a teacher.**

26.2
① he's a farmer
② she's a teacher
③ he's a student
④ she goes to the gym
⑤ he's an actor
⑥ he has the flu
⑦ she's a chef

26.3 ◀))
① Aziz lives in the countryside because **he thinks it's beautiful**.
② We don't have breakfast because **we're very busy**.
③ Mr. Aspinall gets up early because **he takes his dog for a walk**.
④ Arnold wears a suit because **he works in a bank**.
⑤ Vicky works outside because **she is a gardener**.
⑥ I work in a hospital because **I'm a doctor**.

26.4 ◀))
1. Clara works in a theater because she is an actor.
2. Clara lives on a farm because she is a farmer.
3. Clara works in a hotel because she is a receptionist.
4. Mike lives on a farm because he is a farmer.
5. Mike works in a theater because he is an actor.
6. Mike works in a hotel because he is a receptionist.

27

27.1 ◀))
① kitchen
② toilet
③ television
④ house
⑤ closet (US) / wardrobe (UK)
⑥ bathtub
⑦ garage
⑧ bedroom
⑨ apartment block (US) / block of flats (UK)
⑩ couch (US) / sofa (UK)
⑪ shower
⑫ dining room
⑬ door
⑭ window
⑮ table
⑯ chair
⑰ lamp
⑱ refrigerator (US) / fridge (UK)
⑲ study
⑳ bed
㉑ bookcase
㉒ bathroom
㉓ armchair

28

28.1 ◀))
① My friend **has** new glasses.
② John **has** two dogs.
③ We **have** an old castle in our city.

④ They **have** a lot of parks in their town.
⑤ I **have** a beautiful necklace.
⑥ Alex **has** a new camera.
⑦ Our house **has** a lovely yard.
⑧ Phil and Sue **have** four daughters.
⑨ Pete **has** a new cell phone.
⑩ Your town **has** a big hotel.
⑪ I **have** a lot of friends.

28.2 ◀))
① Bob and Shirley **have** a big dog.
② She **has** some new friends.
③ We **have** two sons at home.
④ James **has** two cars.
⑤ His house **has** three bedrooms.
⑥ Pam **has** lots of books at home.
⑦ He **has** two cats.
⑧ Sally's house **has** a new kitchen.
⑨ You **have** a beautiful house.
⑩ I **have** three sisters.
⑪ Kelly and Mark **have** a microwave.
⑫ We **have** a castle in our town.
⑬ Sanjay **has** a cat and a dog.
⑭ You **have** three brothers.
⑮ Ross **has** a new cell phone.
⑯ Our house **has** two bathrooms.
⑰ I **have** a couch in my room.
⑱ Washington **has** some lovely parks.

28.3 ◀))
① I have two sisters.
② You have a beautiful house.
③ We have a garden.
④ Sam and Greg have a dog.
⑤ Marlon has a brother.
⑥ Fardale has an old castle.
⑦ They have a new car.

28.4
① False
② False
③ False
④ True
⑤ False
⑥ False
⑦ True

28.5 ◀))
① We don't have a computer at home.
② My city doesn't have a castle.
③ Rob's house doesn't have a garage.
④ You don't have any sisters.
⑤ The village doesn't have any stores.

28.6 ◀))

1. You have got a beautiful necklace.
2. She has not got any sisters.
3. We have not got a microwave.
4. Greg has not got a bike.
5. My town has got two theaters.
6. Chloe has not got a cat.
7. They have got a new house.

28.7

1. Our town
2. Adam and I
3. Sally and Jonathan
4. My friend Sam
5. Our house

28.8 ◀))

1. I have a computer.
2. I have a sofa.
3. I have some tables.
4. We have a computer.
5. We have a sofa.
6. We have some tables.
7. He has a sofa.
8. He has a computer.
9. He has some tables.
10. He doesn't have a computer.
11. He doesn't have a sofa.

28.9

1. She has two bedrooms.
   She's got two bedrooms.
2. They have not got a dog.
   They haven't got a dog.
3. We have some chairs.
   We have got some chairs.
4. He has a brother.
   He's got a brother.
5. Carla has not got a sister.
   Carla hasn't got a sister.
6. You have a car.
   You've got a car.
7. Phil has a dog.
   Phil has got a dog.
8. You have got a yard.
   You've got a yard.
9. Jamal doesn't have a sofa.
   Jamal has not got a sofa.
10. They have a shower.
    They've got a shower.
11. May has a couch.
    May has got a couch.
12. He has not got a cat.
    He hasn't got a cat.

29

29.1 ◀))

1. fork
2. washing machine
3. kettle
4. toaster
5. refrigerator
6. sink
7. plate

29.2 ◀))

1. Does the house have a yard?
2. Does their kitchen have a refrigerator?
3. Does Bill's house have a big garage?
4. Do you have a sofa?
5. Does Barry have a kettle?
6. Does she have a barbecue at her house?
7. Does Marge have a new washing machine?
8. Do Jack and Marienne have a TV?
9. Does Leela's brother have a knife and fork?

29.3

1. Claudia
2. Paul
3. Jenny
4. Colin
5. Roberto

29.4 ◀))

1. Yes, I do.
2. No, I don't.
3. Yes, I do.
4. Yes, I do.
5. No, I don't.

29.5 ◀))

1. Do you have any chairs?
2. Do you have any knives?
3. Do you have a refrigerator?
4. Does he have any chairs?
5. Does he have any knives?
6. Does he have a refrigerator?
7. Do they have any chairs?
8. Do they have any knives?
9. Do they have a refrigerator?

29.6 ◀))

1. Yes, **she does**.
2. Yes, **he does**.

3. No, **he doesn't**.
4. Yes, **it does**.
5. No, **they don't**.
6. No, **she doesn't**.
7. Yes, **he does**.

29.7 ◀))

1. Have they got a microwave?
2. Have Shaun and Shania got a pet snake?
3. Has Charles got a camera?
4. Has Clarissa got a new laptop?
5. Has Carol's house got a big yard?
6. Have your friends got my book?
7. Has Brian got a new TV?

29.8 ◀))

1. Has the kitchen got a microwave?
2. Has your house got a yard?
3. Have the Hendersons got a car?
4. Has Claire got my glasses?
5. Have your parents got a computer?
6. Has Paul got my book?
7. Has Brian got a magazine?
8. Have your neighbors got a basement?
9. Has your cell phone got a camera?
10. Has Sam got any money?
11. Has your town got a supermarket?
12. Has Brian got a sister?
13. Have your children got a cat?
14. Has your husband got a camera?
15. Has your school got a library?
16. Has Jane got a cell phone?
17. Have the kids got their bikes?

29.9 ◀))

1. Have you got a refrigerator?
2. Have you got a car?
3. Have you got any brothers or sisters?
4. Has John got a refrigerator?
5. Has John got a car?
6. Has John got any brothers or sisters?
7. Has your kitchen got a refrigerator?

30

30.1 ◀))

1. burger
2. spaghetti
3. juice
4. bread
5. fish

6 apple
7 eggs
8 drinks
9 banana
10 seafood
11 milk
12 strawberry
13 chocolate
14 cheese
15 orange
16 cereal
17 potatoes
18 sugar
19 butter
20 salad
21 meat
22 coffee
23 pasta
24 vegetables
25 cake
26 water
27 fruit
28 rice
29 breakfast
30 lunch
31 dinner

31

31.1 ◀))
DÉNOMBRABLES : **apple**, **burger**, **egg**
INDÉNOMBRABLES : **coffee**, **rice**, **juice**

31.2 ◀))
1 There **is** some orange juice.
2 Sam has **some** milk.
3 We have **some** salt.
4 There **are** some apples.
5 Rita has **a** banana.
6 I've got **some** eggs.

31.3 ◀))
1 four bananas
2 two eggs
3 some cheese
4 two burgers
5 one bar of chocolate

31.4
1 There is some salt.
   There isn't any salt.

2 Is there any wine?
   There isn't any wine.
3 There are some burgers.
   There aren't any burgers.
4 Are there any cookies?
   There aren't any cookies.
5 Are there any pastries?
   There are some pastries.
6 There is some bread.
   There isn't any bread.
7 Is there any rice?
   There isn't any rice.
8 Is there any butter?
   There is some butter.
9 There are some pizzas.
   There aren't any pizzas.
10 Is there any cheese?
   There isn't any cheese.

31.5
1 False
2 True
3 False
4 True
5 False
6 True
7 True
8 False
9 False

31.6 ◀))
1 There's a **glass** of milk.
2 There are two **bags** of rice.
3 There's a **bar** of chocolate.
4 There's a **carton** of juice.
5 There are three **bottles** of water.
6 There's a **bowl** of pasta.
7 There are two **cups** of tea.

31.7 ◀))
1 There **is** a jar of coffee.
2 There **isn't** any rice.
3 There **are** two cartons of juice.
4 There **is** some meat.
5 There **are** two bottles of wine.
6 There **isn't** any bread.
7 There **is** a bag of flour.
8 There **is** some pasta.
9 There **are** two bars of chocolate.
10 There **isn't** any sugar.
11 There **is** some butter.

31.8
1 bowl
2 jar
3 bar
4 glass
5 carton
6 bag
7 cup
8 bottle
9 tube

31.9 ◀))
1 How **much** meat is there?
2 How **many** cartons of milk are there?
3 How **many** bowls of rice are there?
4 How **much** juice is there?
5 How **much** bread is there?
6 How **many** cups of tea are there?
7 How **many** bars of chocolate are there?
8 How **much** coffee is there?
9 How **many** jars of jam are there?
10 How **much** milk is there?
11 How **many** bags of flour are there?
12 How **much** pizza is there?
13 How **many** eggs are there?

31.10 ◀))
1. How many burgers are there?
2. How many eggs are there?
3. How many people are there?
4. How much rice is there?
5. How much water is there?
6. How much coffee is there?

32

32.1 ◀))
1 There are **too many** pears.
2 There is **too much** milk.
3 She has **too much** pasta.
4 We have **too many** bananas.
5 There is **too much** butter.
6 There are **too many** apples.
7 There are **too many** tomatoes.
8 I have **too much** juice.
9 There are **too many** mushrooms.
10 They have **too many** burgers.
11 Sue owns **too many** shoes.

32.2 🔊
1. There **are enough** pineapples.
2. There **are enough** mangoes.
3. There **is enough** sugar.
4. There **is enough** bread.
5. There **is enough** milk.
6. There **is enough** pasta.
7. There **are enough** apples.
8. There **are enough** oranges.
9. There **are enough** bananas.
10. There **is enough** chocolate.
11. There **are enough** eggs.
12. There **is enough** cheese.
13. There **are enough** tomatoes.
14. There **is enough** butter.
15. There **is enough** juice.

32.3
1. You have enough oranges.
   You have too many oranges.
2. There isn't enough sugar.
   There's too much sugar.
3. We don't have enough butter.
   We have enough butter.
4. There aren't enough eggs.
   There are too many eggs.
5. There is enough flour.
   There is too much flour.
6. There aren't enough potatoes.
   There are enough potatoes.
7. You don't have enough melons.
   You have too many melons.
8. He has enough bread.
   He has too much bread.
9. There isn't enough tea.
   There is enough tea.
10. We don't have enough milk.
    We have too much milk.
11. You have enough rice.
    You have too much rice.
12. There aren't enough mangoes.
    There are enough mangoes.
13. Martha doesn't have enough onions.
    Martha has too many onions.
14. You have enough carrots.
    You have too many carrots.

32.4
1. True
2. True
3. False
4. False
5. False

32.5 🔊
1. There are **not enough** carrots.
2. There are **enough** potatoes.
3. There are **not enough** tomatoes.
4. There is **not enough** pasta.
5. There is **too much** oil.
6. There is **enough** bread.
7. There is **enough** butter.
8. There is **too much** flour.
9. There is **not enough** sugar.
10. There are **enough** oranges.
11. There are **not enough** bananas.
12. There are **too many** eggs.
13. There is **enough** milk.

32.6 🔊
1. There **isn't** enough butter.
2. There **aren't** enough tomatoes.
3. There **aren't** enough mangoes.
4. You have too **many** bananas.
5. They don't have **enough** butter.
6. There **are** enough onions.
7. There **isn't** enough sugar.
8. You have **too** many pineapples.
9. They have too **much** bread.
10. You **don't** have enough apples.
11. They have **enough** flour.
12. There **are** too many potatoes.
13. There **is** too much salt.
14. There **is** too much chocolate.
15. There **are** too many mangoes.
16. You have **enough** eggs.
17. There **are** enough oranges.

32.7 🔊
1. There is enough butter.
2. There is not enough butter.
3. There is too much butter.
4. There are enough eggs.
5. There are not enough eggs.
6. There are too many eggs.
7. There is enough rice.
8. There is not enough rice.
9. There is too much rice.

33

33.1 🔊
1. gloves
2. hat
3. blue
4. boots
5. jeans
6. pink
7. red
8. suit
9. dress
10. belt
11. coat
12. green
13. skirt
14. shirt
15. black
16. scarf
17. yellow
18. sandals
19. socks
20. purple
21. extra small
22. small
23. medium
24. large
25. extra large
26. orange
27. shoes

34

34.1 🔊
1. That sweater **fits** you. It's the right size.
2. My mom always **chooses** my dad's clothes.
3. These jeans don't **fit**. They're too small.
4. I **own** 30 pairs of shoes.
5. I always **try on** clothes before I buy them.
6. Those shops **sell** very fashionable clothes.
7. We **buy** fruit at the market.
8. I **want** some shoes for my birthday.
9. I sometimes **pay** by credit card.

34.2 🔊
1. Ruth **does** a lot of her shopping on the internet.
2. The shop **doesn't** sell my size of clothes.
3. She **wears** short skirts.
4. Greg's jeans **don't** fit him.
5. Amy **owns** a lot of fashionable clothes.
6. We **pay** for our shopping with cash.
7. Duncan never **tries** on clothes before he buys them.

8 My parents usually **pay** for my clothes.

9 Peter **doesn't** own many clothes.

---

1 That blouse **doesn't** fit you.

2 Sue always **tries** on her new clothes.

3 Rob **wants** a new tie for Christmas.

4 Peter **buys** his meat at the butcher's shop.

5 Jose **owns** a beautiful house in France.

6 My jeans **don't** fit me. They're too big.

7 Samantha **chooses** high-quality clothes.

8 They **sell** vegetables in the market.

9 Do you **want** a new shirt for your birthday?

34.4 🔊

1 This is a **new** T-shirt.

2 These are **short** jeans.

3 This is an **expensive** tie.

4 This is a **large** sweater.

5 This is a **blue** dress.

6 This is an **old** T-shirt.

7 These are **cheap** shoes.

8 This is a **short** skirt.

9 This is a **red** shirt.

10 These are **big** shoes.

11 This is a **small** sweater.

34.5

1 a red skirt

2 a red scarf

3 brown shoes

4 blue jeans

5 green coat.

34.6

1 cheap

2 short

3 long

4 hard

5 soft

34.7 🔊

1 too hard

2 too old

3 too expensive

4 too long

5 too soft

6 too short

34.8 🔊

1 Claire's hat is **too small**.

2 These shoes are **too expensive**.

3 Sophie's pullover is **too small**.

4 Corrine's coat is **big enough**.

5 Emma's sweater is **too big**.

6 Chloe's scarf is **too long**.

7 Phoebe's shoes are **too big**.

8 Joshua's jacket is **too small**.

35

35.1

1 False **2** True **3** True **4** True **5** False **6** True **7** False **8** True **9** False

---

35.2 🔊

1 Our house has a pretty little yard.

2 James has an ugly leather jacket.

3 Pete has an old wooden table.

4 This is a brilliant new book.

5 Shelley's got a beautiful glass bottle.

6 That was such a boring old film.

7 That's an ugly woolen sweater.

8 Those are boring black shoes.

9 I've got a horrible old car.

10 Simone has a beautiful gray parrot.

11 That's a horrible old house!

12 You've got a nice red shirt.

35.3 🔊

1 Jill's got a beautiful black dog.

2 Simon has a nice new house.

3 They have an ugly old car.

4 Those are pretty red shoes.

5 That's an ugly pink hat.

6 Greg has a horrible brown snake.

7 You've got a beautiful black bag.

8 This is a great new book.

35.4

1 metal

2 paper

3 wool

4 glass

5 leather

6 wood

35.5

1 plastic **2** wooden **3** glass **4** leather **5** plastic **6** wool **7** wooden **8** paper **9** wool **10** plastic **11** leather **12** metal **13** metal

---

35.6 🔊

1 Four **plastic** cups.

2 An ugly **wooden** table.

3 An old **leather** jacket.

4 Three **metal** chairs.

5 A green **wool** sweater.

6 A brown **paper** bag.

7 Beautiful **fabric**.

36

36.1 🔊

1 roller-skating

2 rugby

3 golf

4 snowboarding

5 cycling

6 badminton

7 ice hockey

8 baseball

9 skateboarding

10 swimming

11 running

12 basketball

13 tennis

14 skiing

15 horse riding

36.2 🔊

1 baseball bat

2 golf course

3 snowboard

4 swimming pool

5 golf club

6 running track

7 skateboard

8 stadium

9 surfboard

10 tennis court

11 skis

37

37.1 🔊

1 Douglas **goes cycling** with his brother on Sundays.

2 Phil and John **go skating** in the winter.

3 Mr. Henderson **goes sailing** in the Mediterranean in the summer.

4 Veronica **goes dancing** with her friends on the weekend.

5 They **go hiking** in the mountains in Scotland.

6 Lawrence **goes swimming** on Tuesdays.

7 Ted **goes skateboarding** on Saturday morning.

8 I **go horseback riding** in France each year.

9 She **goes shopping** in Milan at Christmas.

10 We **go fishing** after work on Mondays.

11 Anne **goes surfing** in California.

37.2 ◀))

1 Jane goes **dancing** on Friday nights.

2 Our dad goes **sailing** in the summer.

3 I go **fishing** in the evening.

4 Do you go **running** in the morning?

5 They go **cycling** in the summer.

6 Sam goes **swimming** on Sundays.

7 I go **horseback riding** daily.

8 Claire goes **shopping** in London.

9 Omar goes **skateboarding** daily.

10 Do you go **dancing** with her?

11 Rachel goes **hiking** in Peru.

12 I go **snowboarding** in the winter.

13 Bob and Steve go **surfing** in Tahiti.

37.3 ◀))

1 snowboarding
2 running
3 fishing
4 swimming
5 skateboarding
6 dancing
7 surfing
8 shopping
9 cycling
10 sailing
11 riding

37.4 ◀))

1 I **go** shopping in the evening.

2 Jan **goes** skateboarding on Fridays.

3 Pete **goes** sailing on the weekend.

4 Sam **goes** skating every December.

5 I **go** running on Wednesday.

6 They **go** fishing with their friends.

7 Sarah **goes** dancing on Saturdays.

37.5 ◀))

1 Do you **play** chess?

2 Paolo **plays** badminton at the weekend.

3 My father **plays** golf with his friends.

4 We **don't play** baseball anymore.

5 I **play** tennis with my brother.

6 Greg **doesn't play** basketball.

7 Liz **plays** racquet ball on the weekend.

8 Your dad **doesn't play** soccer.

9 Our dog **plays** with its ball.

10 Mike **plays** soccer on Saturdays.

11 We **don't play** golf in the winter.

12 Pammy **doesn't play** tennis.

37.6 ◀))

1 Does he play badminton on Fridays?

2 Does Noah play golf with his grandpa?

3 Do they play basketball with their friends?

4 Does Georgia play baseball at school?

5 Do we play tennis in the summer?

6 Do Tim's parents play chess in the evening?

37.7

1 False **2** True **3** False **4** True
5 False **6** True **7** True

37.8 ◀))

1 John **plays** badminton on Wednesday.

2 You **go** fishing with your brother.

3 My uncle **plays** chess with my aunt.

4 We **go** dancing in the evening.

5 Sally's dad **plays** rugby.

6 Bartou **goes** cycling in the mountains.

7 Ramona **plays** racquet ball with her dad.

8 Our kids **play** baseball after school.

9 Simon and Pam **go** surfing in the summer.

10 They **play** basketball every Saturday.

11 We **go** snowboarding in Austria.

37.9 ◀))

1 I **play baseball** with my friends at school.

2 Anna **goes skateboarding** in the afternoon on Sundays.

3 Mrs. Amir **plays chess** with her husband in the evening.

4 Max **plays badminton** on Tuesdays and Fridays.

5 Peter **goes fishing** with his brother on Mondays and Wednesdays.

38

38.1 ◀))

1 play a musical instrument

2 write
3 do yoga
4 play video games
5 watch television
6 walk / hike
7 go the gym
8 sew
9 go shopping
10 do the gardening
11 draw
12 go camping
13 bake
14 listen to music
15 do puzzles
16 watch a movie
17 visit a museum
18 play cards
19 see a play
20 meet friends
21 knit
22 paint
23 read
24 go bird watching
25 go out for a meal
26 play chess
27 take photos

39

39.1

1 True **2** False **3** False **4** False
5 True **6** False **7** True

39.2 ◀))

1 They sometimes go to the theater.

2 Mike never goes running after work.

3 You always go to bed early.

4 Jane often goes shopping on Saturday.

5 We usually eat dinner at 6pm.

39.3

1 never **2** sometimes **3** often
4 usually **5** always **6** often

39.4 ◀))

1 Clara **never** plays chess with her grandfather.

2 Enzo **always** eats chocolate ice cream.

3 Paul **sometimes** goes fishing in the morning.

4 My parents **usually** drive to work.

5 Gill **never** goes shopping with her mom.

6 You **sometimes** go to the gym in the town.

7 Shelley **usually** watches TV in the evening.

8 My dog **always** sleeps under the table.

9 We **sometimes** play baseball in the summer.

10 Tim **usually** rides his horse on the weekend.

39.5 🔊

1 How often does Steph watch TV?

2 How often do you visit your dad?

3 When do they play soccer?

4 When do you usually go to bed?

5 How often does May go running?

6 How often do you play tennis?

7 How often does Jo read a book?

39.6 🔊

1 **She goes to the gym** on Wednesdays.

2 **He plays soccer** in the evening.

3 She never **goes to the theater**.

4 He sometimes **reads a newspaper**.

5 **She visits her family** four times a year.

6 **He plays baseball** every afternoon.

7 **She goes shopping** twice a week.

8 **I read** a book every evening.

9 She sometimes **makes a cake**.

39.7 🔊

1 How often does Jimmy play soccer?

2 How often do you phone your grandma?

3 How often does Sheila get up at 7am?

4 How often do you read a book?

5 How often does Sally go to work?

6 How often do you play badminton?

7 How often does your daughter go running?

8 How often does Megan go fishing?

9 How often do you watch TV?

39.8 🔊

1 She always **goes** dancing on the weekend.

2 I often **go** fishing.

3 My mom never **gets up** early.

4 Seb usually **plays** soccer on weekends.

5 Tracy never **watches** TV in the evening.

6 We sometimes **take** the bus to work.

7 Doug often **plays** tennis on Fridays.

40

40.1 🔊

1 We like cake.

2 I hate tennis.

3 We love basketball.

4 Shelley loves pizza.

5 They hate board games.

6 I don't like pasta.

7 Samantha likes chocolate.

40.2

1 salad **2** sports **3** playing tennis **4** golf
5 listening to music **6** classical music
7 going shopping **8** going to the cinema
9 scary films **10** taking photos

40.3 🔊

1 Chris doesn't like spiders.

2 They hate Paris.

3 Mrs. McGregor doesn't like cats.

4 We hate soccer.

5 We don't like wine.

6 Simone hates her horse.

7 He doesn't like your necklace.

8 Jean-Marie hates sports.

9 Colin doesn't like pizza.

10 Douglas doesn't like Anne.

11 Cynthia loves dogs.

12 We hate chocolate.

13 You don't like cheese.

14 Susan doesn't like pizza.

40.4 🔊

1. They love cats.

2. They love running.

3. They love pizza.

4. They love snakes.

5. Arnold hates cats.

6. Arnold hates running.

7. Arnold hates pizza.

8. Arnold hates snakes.

9. My mother hates cats.

10. My mother hates running.

11. My mother hates pizza.

12. My mother hates snakes.

40.5

1 She likes cooking.

2 Her favorite is Italian food.

3 She doesn't like cooking meat.

4 She cooks for her friends and family.

5 She doesn't like fast food.

6 She hates candy.

40.6 🔊

1 I **hate** cities, but I **love** the country.

2 Archie **likes** ice cream, and he **loves** pizza.

3 He **loves** meat, but he **hates** fish.

4 Francis **doesn't like** coffee, but he **likes** tea.

5 We **hate** Mondays, but we **love** Fridays.

6 My dad **dislikes** classical music, but he **loves** rock.

40.7 🔊

1 Sam likes watching soccer **because it's exciting.**

2 Marie loves pizza. **She thinks it's delicious.**

3 I love reading history books **because they're really interesting.**

4 Sally doesn't like running **because it is tiring.**

5 Peggy does not like eating meat **because she is a vegetarian.**

6 Paolo does not eat chocolate **because he doesn't have a sweet tooth.**

7 Jemma hates snakes. **She thinks they are scary.**

40.8

1 hot

2 interesting

3 delicious

4 boring

5 tiring

41

41.1 🔊

1 sing a song

2 dance

3 electric guitar

4 headphones

5 opera

6 keyboard

7 piano

8 rap

9 country

10 album

11 rock

12 guitar
13 Latin
14 orchestra
15 jazz
16 flute
17 conductor
18 saxophone
19 audience
20 guitar player
21 play the trumpet
22 trumpet
23 concert
24 violin
25 drum
26 microphone
27 harmonica

42

42.1 🔊
1 Nick's favorite uncle is an actor.
2 Jo's favorite book is *Puzzling People*.
3 Jay's favorite instrument is the piano.
4 Paul's favorite drink is orange juice.
5 Blake's favorite animal is the tiger.
6 Dan's favorite place is his garden.
7 Sanjay's favorite season is winter.
8 Max's favorite hobby is painting.
9 Greg's favorite food is rice.
10 Levi's favorite sport is baseball.
11 Martha's favorite country is France.
12 Simone's favorite lesson is science.
13 Maya's favorite dessert is cake.
14 Karina's favorite fruit is pineapple.
15 Their favorite city is London.
16 Kate's favorite pet is her parrot.
17 Zoe's favorite pastime is dancing.

42.2
1 math
2 Friday
3 red
4 chocolate cake
5 baseball
6 fall

42.3 🔊
1 Barbara likes listening to music in the evening.
2 Arnold's favorite food is ice cream and pizza.
3 Craig doesn't like getting up in the morning.
4 Seb's favorite type of music is hip-hop.
5 Ruth likes orange juice.
6 Daniel's favorite animal is the lion.
7 I like bacon and eggs for breakfast.
8 Aziz doesn't like lasagna or spaghetti.
9 Miguel loves going to the movie theater.

42.4
1 True 2 False 3 False 4 False
5 True 6 False 7 False 8 True 9 True
10 True

42.5 🔊
1 Arnie's favorite sport is **tennis**.
2 Joan's favorite animal is a **dolphin**.
3 Hassan's favorite actor is **Chris Minota**.
4 Pam's favorite number is **21**.
5 Jane's favorite sport is **badminton**.
6 Dora's favorite ice cream is **strawberry**.
7 Jim's favorite food is **spaghetti**.

42.6 🔊
1. She loves salsa dancing.
2. She loves sailing.
3. She loves chocolate ice cream.
4. Simon loves salsa dancing.
5. Simon loves sailing.
6. Simon loves chocolate ice cream.
7. She likes salsa dancing.
8. She likes sailing.
9. She likes chocolate ice cream.
10. Simon likes salsa dancing.
11. Simon likes sailing.
12. Simon likes chocolate ice cream.
13. Her favorite food is chocolate ice cream.
14. Her favorite sport is sailing.

43

43.1 🔊
1 talk
2 shout
3 throw
4 listen
5 lift
6 hit
7 walk
8 add
9 kick
10 make (a snowman)
11 carry
12 fly
13 sit
14 act
15 see
16 do (homework)
17 ride
18 catch
19 spell
20 move
21 stand up
22 understand
23 jump
24 climb
25 subtract
26 drive
27 work

44

44.1
1 I can ride a horse.
  I can't ride a horse.
2 I cannot climb a tree.
  I can't climb a tree.
3 I can speak French.
  I cannot speak French.
4 I can sing.
  I can't sing.
5 I can lift a box.
  I cannot lift a box.
6 I can fly a kite.
  I can't fly a kite.
7 I cannot catch a fish.
  I can't catch a fish.
8 I can swim.
  I can't swim.

44.2 🔊
1 Kate **can hit** the ball.
2 Paul **can't do** math.
3 Helen **can spell** very well.
4 Ivan **can't run** very fast.
5 Sara **can move** the chair.
6 Alex **can't play** badminton.
7 Lynn **can ride** a bicycle.

44.3 🔊
1 Eliza cannot drive a car.
2 Jonathan can play the piano.

3 Cathy can't jump very high.
4 Mick can throw a stick.
5 Laura can't do math.
6 Alan can lift the box.
7 Julia can't swim very far.

44.4
1 Can **2** Can't **3** Can't **4** Can **5** Can

44.5 🔊
1 Can Maria and Juan spell English words?
2 Can the children do their math homework?
3 Can you sing difficult jazz songs?
4 Can Mark ride a horse?
5 Can Jack climb a tree?
6 Can he carry that box?
7 Can Carlos kick a football?
8 Can Adam and Ella dance the tango?
9 Can Peter and John swim?

44.6 🔊
1 Jack is a diving teacher. He can **swim very well**.
2 Carla lives on a farm. She can **ride a horse** and look after animals.
3 Bobby is good at languages. He can **speak Russian**.
4 Nuna likes going on winter vacations. She can **ski well**.
5 Jim is a great children's teacher. He can **tell stories** well.

44.7 🔊
1 Yes, **I can**. **2** No, **I can't**. **3** Yes, **I can**.
4 No, **I can't**. **5** No, **I can't**. **6** Yes, **I can**.
7 No, **I can't**. **8** No, **I can't**. **9** No, **I can't**.
10 Yes, **I can**. **11** Yes, **I can**.

44.8 🔊
1. I can ride a bicycle.
2. I can't ride a bicycle.
3. She can ride a bicycle.
4. She can't ride a bicycle.
5. They can ride a bicycle.
6. They can't ride a bicycle.
7. I can swim a mile.
8. I can't swim a mile.
9. She can swim a mile.
10. She can't swim a mile.
11. They can swim a mile.
12. They can't swim a mile.
13. I can play tennis.
14. I can't play tennis.

15. She can play tennis.
16. She can't play tennis.
17. They can play tennis.
18. They can't play tennis.

45

45.1 🔊
1 My friend speaks too **quietly**.
2 A turtle walks very **slowly**.
3 Alan can speak German **well**.
4 My dog can run very **fast**.
5 I get up very **early**.

45.2
1 Patrick is good at dancing.
2 Caitlin bakes well.
3 My mother is good at writing.
4 Ethan plays the guitar well.
5 Aimee is good at skiing.
6 They swim well.
7 We are good at speaking English.
8 Lara climbs trees well.

45.3 🔊
1 Haruda sometimes arrives **late** for school.
2 My cousin Paul runs **quickly**.
3 Shelley sings **beautifully**.
4 Our neighbors talk so **noisily** at night.
5 Rosa reads very **slowly**.
6 I can pass this exam **easily**.
7 My aunt drives very **carefully**.
8 Anita works very **hard**.
9 We **usually** go to bed at 11pm.
10 Angela speaks English **badly**.
11 A cheetah runs very **fast**.
12 Sarah eats her food very **quickly**.
13 Andrew does his homework **well**.

45.4 🔊
1. I am good at drawing.
2. I am good at playing the drums.
3. I am good at English.
4. I am bad at drawing.
5. I am bad at playing the drums.
6. I am bad at English.
7. Jennifer is good at drawing.
8. Jennifer is good at playing the drums.
9. Jennifer is good at English.
10. Jennifer is bad at drawing.
11. Jennifer is bad at playing the drums.

12. Jennifer is bad at English.
13. We are good at drawing.
14. We are good at playing the drums.
15. We are good at English.
16. We are bad at drawing.
17. We are bad at playing the drums.
18. We are bad at English.

46

46.1 🔊
1 Pedro is really good at history.
2 You speak French really well.
3 Sandra is very good at singing.
4 Sal is quite good at skiing.
5 Your uncle can swim very well.
6 They can run quite fast.
7 Mr. Henderson is really good at golf.

46.2 🔊
1 Arnold isn't very good at art and design.
2 My cousin is really good at speaking English.
3 Jean is quite good at climbing mountains.

46.3
1 My aunt is quite good at speaking Polish.
2 Your brother surfs really well.
3 Katie paints very well.
4 Silvia is really good at singing.
5 Martina is very good at dancing.
6 Serge cooks quite well.
7 Sonia is really good at playing chess.
8 Ricky runs very well.
9 Peter is quite good at drawing.
10 My mom speaks Greek really well.
11 David is very good at playing the drums.

46.4 🔊
1 Charlotte can ski quite well.
2 Harry sings really quietly.
3 My aunt walks very slowly.
4 Elizabeth speaks Russian very well.
5 My dog can jump quite high.
6 William speaks Japanese really badly.
7 Philip eats quite noisily.

47

47.1
1. She wants to have a cat.
   She'd like to have a cat.
2. They would like to visit Tokyo.
   They'd like to visit Tokyo.
3. I want to eat an orange.
   I would like to eat an orange.
4. You want to learn Spanish.
   You'd like to learn Spanish.
5. We want to go to a café.
   We would like to go to a café.
6. He would like to live in Germany.
   He'd like to live in Germany.
7. We want to swim in a lake.
   We'd like to swim in a lake.

47.2 ◀))
1. They'd like to go sailing on a sailboat.
2. Dan would like to travel to New York.
3. Sharon wants to read her book.
4. Doug would like to climb a mountain.
5. We want to go on vacation to Tahiti.

47.3 ◀))
1. Douglas wants to have pasta.
2. They'd like to go home tomorrow.
3. Does Chris want to go swimming later?
4. Sheila doesn't want to see Paul.
5. Would you like to visit us tomorrow?
6. Our children want to go to college.
7. She'd like to buy a new cell phone.
8. Jenny wants to go shopping on Friday.
9. Simon would like to be a doctor.
10. I would like to have a hamburger.
11. Would you like to be a vet?
12. Chloe doesn't want to eat that pizza.
13. Do you want to read this book?
14. They would like to watch TV.
15. She wants to go to the party.

47.4 ◀))
1. I'd like to drive around America.
2. I'd like to travel around America.
3. We want to drive around America.
4. We want to travel around America.
5. Greg wants to drive around America.
6. Greg wants to travel around America.
7. I'd like to drive to Miami.
8. I'd like to travel to Miami.
9. We want to drive to Miami.

10. We want to travel to Miami.
11. Greg wants to drive to Miami.
12. Greg wants to travel to Miami.

47.5
1. Yes, he would.
2. No, he doesn't.
3. Yes, he would.
4. Yes, she does.
5. No, she doesn't.
6. No, he doesn't.
7. Yes, she does.

47.6 ◀))
1. Marie wants to go snowboarding in Austria.
2. Mario doesn't want to go to school today.
3. She wants to climb that mountain.
4. Tony would like to play golf in Scotland.

47.7 ◀))
1. Do you want **to** go home now?
2. Claude would **like** to learn French.
3. He would **like** to go swimming.
4. Paolo wants **to** get a new cat.
5. Would you like **to** visit China?
6. **He'd** like to go to work later today.
7. Peter **wants** to go to college next year.
8. They **don't** want to go to school today.
9. My sister **wants** to go to Greece this summer.

47.8 ◀))
1. Would Peter like to go fishing?
2. Does Marion want to play tennis on Saturday?
3. Would he like to visit India?
4. Would Mr. Evans like to play chess tonight?
5. Would you like to play squash this evening?
6. Does Sam want to go to the park again?
7. Would they like to travel around China?

48

48.1 ◀))
1. My mother would really like to travel to Spain.
2. Doug would quite like to learn French.
3. Sally would quite like to do an art degree.

4. Don's brother would like to practice the piano.
5. I'd really like to go to a rock concert tonight.
6. Martha would like to study chemistry in college.
7. My kids would quite like to study German at school.

48.2 ◀))
1. Edith would really like to read her new book.
2. They'd really like to go to a concert.
3. I'd really like to go to France on vacation.
4. Jean-Paul would quite like to speak to you.
5. We'd quite like to eat pizza tonight.
6. Jeremy would really like to play his piano.
7. They'd really like to pass their chemistry exam.
8. Sophie would quite like to speak Mandarin.
9. David would really like to visit his son.

48.3 ◀))
1. I'd really like to improve my English.
2. I'd really like to learn Japanese.
3. I'd really like to do a history degree.
4. I'd quite like to improve my English.
5. I'd quite like to learn Japanese.
6. I'd quite like to do a history degree.
7. Sam would really like to learn Japanese.
8. Sam would really like to do a history degree.
9. Sam would quite like to learn Japanese.
10. Sam would quite like to do a history degree.
11. We'd really like to learn Japanese.
12. We'd really like to do a history degree.
13. We'd quite like to learn Japanese.
14. We'd quite like to do a history degree.

48.4
1. history
2. review
3. music
4. study
5. drama
6. math
7. degree
8. exams

48.5 ◀))
1. Phillipa goes to **college**.
2. Rome is **a beautiful city**.
3. We are at **home** at the moment.

4 Sharon goes to **school** at 9am.
5 **The college** is far away.
6 Peter goes **to bed** at 10pm.
7 My uncle is at **the mosque** today.
8 Jim goes to **church** on Sundays.
9 Sean leaves **home** at 7:30am.
10 Seb lives next to **the hospital**.

48.6 ◀))
1 Carol leaves work at 6pm every day.
2 Jane can drive you to school tomorrow.
3 Chris lives across from the hospital.
4 Carl is at home at the moment.
5 Julia has a beautiful horse.
6 The hospital isn't very far.
7 We go to bed at 11pm usually.
8 Ottersley is a beautiful town.
9 Your shoes are under the bed.

48.7 ◀))
1 Sally is **in hospital**. She is ill.
2 York is **a** pretty town.
3 She is **at home** now.
4 Lizzie goes **to church** on Sundays.
5 Bob is **at work** at the moment.
6 Christopher has **a** new car.
7 Jim goes **to bed** early on Sundays.
8 Carlos is **a** very talented boy.
9 Sarah and John are **a** great team.
10 Mary **bought three** new pens.
11 He jumped into **the** water and started swimming.
12 New York is **a** beautiful city.
13 **The** children were playing in the sun.
14 I can't **play soccer** on Monday.
15 Can you play **the** classical guitar?

48.8
1 Sarah
2 Eddie
3 Robert
4 Oliver

Remerciements

Les éditeurs souhaitent remercier :
Jo Kent, Trish Burrow et Emma Watkins pour le texte supplémentaire ; Thomas Booth, Helen Fanthorpe, Helen Leech, Carrie Lewis et Vicky Richards pour leur assistance rédactionnelle ; Stephen Bere, Sarah Hilder, Amy Child, Fiona Macdonald et Simon Murrell pour le travail de conception supplémentaire ; Simon Mumford pour les cartes et drapeaux nationaux ; Peter Chrisp pour la vérification des faits ; Penny Hands, Amanda Learmonth et Carrie Lewis pour la relecture ; Elizabeth Wise pour l'indexation ; Tatiana Boyko, Rory Farrell, Clare Joyce et Viola Wang pour les illustrations complémentaires ; Liz Hammond pour le montage des scripts et la gestion des enregistrements audio ; Hannah Bowen et Scarlett O'Hara pour la compilation des scripts audio ; Heather Hughes, Tommy Callan, Tom Morse, Gillian Reid et Sonia Charbonnier pour leur soutien créatif et technique ; Priyanka Kharbanda, Suefa Lee, Shramana Purkayastha, Isha Sharma, Sheryl Sadana pour leur assistance rédactionnelle ; Yashashvi Choudhary, Jaileen Kaur, Bhavika Mathur, Richa Verma, Ankita Yadav, Apurva Agarwal pour leur support de conception ; Deepak Negi et Nishwan Rasool pour la recherche d'images ; Rohan Sinha pour le soutien managérial et moral.

Toutes les images sont la propriété de DK. Pour plus d'informations, rendez-vous sur **www.dkimages.com.**